this isn't
the life I signed
up for

Books by
Donna Partow

Becoming a Vessel God Can Use

Becoming the Woman God Wants Me to Be

Becoming the Woman I Want to Be

Living in Absolute Freedom

Standing Firm

This Isn't the Life I Signed Up For

DONNA PARTOW

this isn't the life I signed up for

. . . But I'm Finding Hope and Healing

A TEN-WEEK JOURNEY

BETHANY HOUSE PUBLISHERS

Minneapolis, Minnesota

Published by Bethany House Publishers
11400 Hampshire Avenue South
Bloomington, Minnesota 55438

Bethany House Publishers is a division of
Baker Publishing Group, Grand Rapids, Michigan

Printed in the United States of America

Library of Congress Cataloging-in-Publication Data

Partow, Donna.
    This isn't the life I signed up for : but I'm finding hope and healing, a 10-week journey / Donna Partow.
        p. cm.
    Summary: "In a format that includes study questions for individuals or groups, Donna Partow shows women that no matter how life has disappointed them, God can bring hope and healing where there has been suffering or pain"—Provided by publisher.
    "This isn't the life I signed up for growth guide, formerly published separately (2003), has been incorporated into this book"—T.p. verso.
    ISBN 978-0-7642-0791-4 (pbk. : alk. paper) 1. Christian women—Religious life. 2. Spiritual life—Christianity. I. Title.
    BV4527.P3795   2010
    248.8'43—dc22
                                       2010004416

DONNA PARTOW is a Christian communicator with a compelling testimony of God's transforming power. Her uncommon transparency and passion for Christ have been used by God at women's conferences, retreats and leadership events worldwide. She is the bestselling author of numerous books and has been a popular guest on more than two hundred radio and TV programs, including *Focus on the Family*.

If your church sponsors an annual women's conference or retreat, perhaps they would be interested in learning more about the author's special weekend programs. She is also available for luncheons and one-day events. For more information, see her Web site: *www.donnapartow.com*.

ACKNOWLEDGMENTS

I would like to acknowledge the assistance of the following women, who gave valuable insight into the book you hold in your hands:

The Apron Gang, Vermillion, OH
Barbara Byrd
Sandy Cullum
Sheila Feltner
Ann Flaherty
Becky Freeman
Jeanne Helstrom
Rhoni Kaastra
Kathy Lee
Suzy Manning
Cindy Measel
Angela Patton
Brenda Ponceroff
Patti Shadbolt
Donna Van Buren
Lorie Walton
Kendra Brown Wilder

Nancy Baccaro
Ginny Bass
Lynn Cheetham
Dr. Brenda Cusack
Jacque Fewkes
Lynne Ford
Debbie Gilbert
Stephanie Janke
Chris Khamlin
Judy Link
Pat McBeth
Yvonne Ortega
Tracie Peterson
Joanne Richards
Connie Smith
Marjorie Vawter
Sabrina White
Trudy Wolcott

Eileen Banks
Noreen Boone
Elisa Chung
Loreen Desrosiers
Betty Fitch
Debby France
Cindy Heflin
Cheryl Jones
Vicki J. Kuyper
Deborah Lovett
Carolyn McIntyre
Gail Padilla
Melissa Polley
Lecia Segaard
Helen Stellwag
Denise Walker
Shari Wiegel

My heartfelt thanks to each one of you for your creativity, wisdom, and willingness to "tell it like it is!"

CONTENTS

How to Use This Book for Study   *11*

  1. I Didn't Sign Up for This Life   *17*

  2. I Didn't Sign Up for a Painful Childhood   *35*

  3. I Didn't Sign Up for Disappointing Relationships   *59*

  4. I Didn't Sign Up to Make Foolish Choices   *79*

  5. I Didn't Sign Up for Disappointment With God   *111*

  6. I Signed Up for Happiness   *141*

  7. I Signed Up for Great Health   *161*

  8. I Signed Up for Love   *187*

  9. I Signed Up for the Perfect Little Family   *207*

10. I Signed Up to Make a Difference   *235*

A Note to Leaders   *253*

Discussion Leader's Guide   *257*

Memory Verse Cards   *271*

Affirmation Cards   *275*

How to Use This Book for Study

Reading a book won't necessarily change your life, but *praying through* and *working through* a book most definitely will.

It is possible to work through this book, using the Growth Guide found at the end of each chapter, in your own personal devotional time. However, you will gain far more insight and increase your likelihood of experiencing lasting change if you work through the material with a trusted friend, a small group, or as part of a weekly women's Bible study. There is strength in numbers and power in accountability. If you aren't part of an established group, be bold enough to pick up the phone and make a few calls. No doubt you are surrounded by women who feel trapped in the middle of "the life they didn't sign up for." You may be doing them one of the greatest favors of their lives by inviting them to join you on your journey to hope and healing.

Each week of your journey will include the following components to accompany your reading of the book:

KEY VERSES

I have selected one or two verses that tie in with the chapter theme. I encourage you to choose one each week to memorize.

To facilitate that process, you will find cards at the back of the book. I encourage you to cut these out and tuck them into your purse. Whenever you have a free moment, pull them out and review them. Also in the back of the book you will find Affirmation cards, or personalized Scripture passages (as explained in chapter 6). These are designed specifically for daily recitation and ideally should be read aloud.

KEY POINTS TO REMEMBER

If you have read the corresponding chapter, these key points will serve to refresh your memory about the most important material covered. If you didn't have an opportunity to read the chapter (perhaps you had a hectic week), these points will serve as your *CliffsNotes* to prepare for your small group time! The key points will provide an introduction to the concepts and a springboard into the application questions and other activities.

APPLICATION QUESTIONS

This is the heart of the study. It's your opportunity to reflect upon what you've learned, while learning more about yourself in the process. If you are participating in a group study, it is vital that you spend time seriously considering the questions posed, as they will form the basis of your group discussion. You owe it to yourself—and to the other women traveling this journey with you—to be fully prepared to contribute to the dialogue. If you are pressed for time in preparing for your class, focus your attention on this area first. Although I highly recommend that you read the associated chapter first, I've tried to design the questions so that you CAN answer them simply by reviewing the bulleted Key Points.

Some groups have gone so far as to say, "If you haven't

answered the questions *in writing*, we are still glad you came. You can share your prayer requests, listen attentively to what other women have gleaned from the study, and enjoy the fellowship. However, we ask that you not join in the discussion time." This may seem harsh, but it might be the spur some women need to come prepared. I will leave it up to each group to decide how they want to handle those who come unprepared.

DIGGING DEEPER

This section is for the serious Bible students out there. I would consider this optional but extremely beneficial. Some weeks you may have time to dig deeper—and you'll always be glad you did. But I completely understand that there will probably be other occasions when you may not be able to invest as much time in independent study. Therefore, the material covered in this section will NOT be included in your group discussion.

WORKING IT INTO YOUR LIFE

Now the proverbial rubber meets the road. In this section, you'll have the opportunity to put what you are learning into action in the real world. Each chapter will have at least one practical assignment or a suggested step you can take to move closer to experiencing the life you DID sign up for!

REWRITE ONE OF THIS WEEK'S KEY VERSES

I truly believe one of the best ways to memorize Scripture is to write it out. This space is provided for you to write (and rewrite if space allows) your favorite verse of the week. Don't leave this space blank! I would even encourage you to take this process one step further. Purchase Post-it Notes and rewrite the verse again (perhaps multiple times) and stick them all over your house—especially in places where you are most likely to be staring into space! (I'll leave it to your imagination to figure out where those places might be.)

Here's a tip I've mentioned in previous books to which readers have responded well: Write out the first letter of each word in the verse on an index card, Post-it Note, or slip of paper. Walk away for a while, then come back and see if you can fill in the words of the verse using only the first letters as your clues. Don't ask me why, but this really seems to work!

YOUR PRAYER IN RESPONSE

Space has been provided for you to write out a prayer in response to what God has shown you in your study time. Again, I strongly encourage you to avail yourself of the space provided to practice the vital spiritual discipline of prayer journaling. It is my hope and prayer that you will want to write even more than the space provided allows—and that this study will be a springboard toward full-fledged prayer journaling. That's because prayer journaling is one of the most powerful tools for spiritual cleansing, hearing the voice of God, and finding hope and healing.

If you are in a small group, your leader may ask for volunteers to share their written prayers with the class. This is not a requirement, but I believe it will be a blessing to all involved.

CLOSING PRAYER

For those of you who enjoy guided prayer, I have included a brief prayer to conclude each chapter's study. These are from my heart, and I pray they will bless your heart as well.

So there you have it: your guide to using the study portion

of this book! Please visit my Web site, *www.donnapartow.com*, for support material including video, audio, and live online teaching to supplement your classroom teaching. I pray that this material will move you far along the journey to finding hope and healing.

> Blessings,
> Donna Partow

I didn't sign up for this life

I Didn't Sign Up for This Life

> This day I call heaven and earth as witnesses against you that
> I have set before you life and death, blessings and curses. Now
> choose life, so that you and your children may live and that
> you may love the Lord your God, listen to his voice, and hold
> fast to him.
>
> Deuteronomy 30:19–20

I have a recurring nightmare.

I'm in college, sitting down to take a final exam, when I suddenly realize, "Hey, I never signed up for this class!" The exam is on biochemistry or nuclear physics, when I thought I had signed up for basket weaving. What I assumed would be a no-brainer turns into the ultimate test. Everyone else seems to be zipping along, while I stare blankly at the first problem. *They're making it look so easy*, I think to myself. Waves of fear and insecurity sweep over me as the reality dawns that I am completely unprepared.

Sometimes life can feel like that. We suddenly find ourselves faced with a challenging exam—like cancer, a prodigal child, or the loss of a loved one. We want to cry out, "Hey, God, this isn't the life I signed up for! I *specifically remember* signing up for great parents, a great marriage, and great kids who rise up and call me blessed. I signed up for lifelong friendships, thin thighs, and vibrant health. Instead, I find myself in the middle of a life I DIDN'T sign up for. My husband says he doesn't love me anymore. My daughter just pierced her tongue. The bills are stacked a mile high, and my company just announced another round of layoffs. To top it all off, I'm forty pounds overweight and my doctor says I'm a heart attack waiting to happen."

Can we be honest? Was there ever a time in your life when you said the following prayer: *Dear God, My life is going way too smoothly right now. Could you please arrange for me to get in a car accident so I can suffer from a severe back injury?* Or maybe you've prayed this one: *Thank you, Lord, for allowing me to get pregnant, but do me a favor: complicate the delivery or make sure my child is born with serious health problems.*

What? You never prayed those prayers? Do you know anyone who has?

The obvious truth is: No one asks for the challenges of life. But in the real world, tough times are inevitable. We all want to live happily ever after. Since you've picked up this book, I'm guessing that in one way or another you've encountered a few bumps on the road to bliss. Believe me—I know exactly how you feel.

IS GOD TRYING TO TEACH ME A LESSON?

I originally planned to title this book *God, Please Don't Teach Me Anything Else . . . I Really Don't Want to Know.* When you're going through tough times, people love to *comfort* you with reassuring words about how it will build your character and how you're learning important life lessons. I want to say, "You know, I'm pretty content with my character right where it is. And I already know everything I want to know: like how to drive through McDonald's for a vanilla milk shake when someone hurts my feelings and how to avoid working on deadlines by calling my mom. With Oreos in one hand and a chocolate-covered doughnut in the other, I'm prepared to face whatever life can dish out." Are you with me?

I recently shared this life-concept with my spiritual mentor, who was unimpressed. "Now, Donna," she said in a voice usually reserved for the students in her first-grade class. "You know you don't really mean that. You know you want to learn all that God has for you so you can become the person he wants you to be." Then she explained that an easy life is not necessarily a good life and a good life is rarely easy. I know she's right, but wouldn't it be great if there *were* an easier way? Wouldn't you like to get a PhD in the School of Life without ever taking a challenging class? Imagine if you never had to face adversity, never had to make any tough choices, and never had to live with the painful consequences of other people's choices.

First you make your choices; then your choices make you.

In reality, choices are the stuff of life. First you make your choices; then your choices make you. This is how the Bible puts it:

> This day I call heaven and earth as witnesses against you that I have set before you life and death, blessings and curses. Now choose life, so that you and your children may live and that you may love the Lord your God, listen to his voice, and hold fast to him. (Deuteronomy 30:19–20)

So basically, we human beings take a multiple-choice exam every day of our lives. The choices are always the same:

   a. Choose life.
   b. Choose death.
   c. Refuse to make a choice (in itself a choice).
   d. Go back and forth between "a" and "b."

Of course, all the while God is saying to us, *"The correct choice is 'a.' Your life will be so much better if you choose 'a.' "*

It might seem that life would be easier if God would do the choosing for us. Eve could have passed the first exam with flying colors if God had reached down into the garden of Eden, grabbed her grasping fingers, and prevented her from picking the forbidden fruit. In the same way, God could have prevented your husband from choosing to make his career a higher priority than your family. He could have prevented your teenager from getting into that car with a bunch of drunken friends.

God could have created a world filled with flawless humans who always choose what is right, but he already had an entire universe teeming with created things that had no choice but to honor him. The stars in the sky *must* obey him and the planets *must* remain in their appointed orbits. The flowers in the field *must* show forth his glory. The oceans *must* proclaim his power and majesty. The birds of the air and the animals that fill the earth *must* illustrate his beauty and creativity. They cannot do otherwise.

We are the only created beings who get to choose how we will respond to God and the world around us. We are the only creatures facing that multiple-choice exam with a pencil in our hand and the power to say, *"God, I know what you want me to do, but I'm going to choose the opposite anyway. I'm going with 'b' and you can't stop me."* It was a risky move on his part to create humans as free moral agents. God knew that from the beginning, but he willingly opened himself up to the pain of rejection. He is indeed grieved when people choose to disobey and dishonor him, but God doesn't force himself on anyone. I believe he finds more joy in one person who *chooses* to love him—and to keep on loving him even in the face of adversity—than he finds in all the beauty of every other created thing combined.

Perhaps you have experienced a major tragedy. Or maybe you are simply overwhelmed by the accumulated weight of one disappointment after another. You can't always control what happens to you, but you can choose how you will respond. You can say, "This isn't the life I signed up for, and I refuse to accept how things have turned out. I'm going to stay stuck in this place of pain forever and no one can stop me." Or you can declare, "This isn't the life I signed up for, and I'm absolutely heartbroken about it. But I know I have to move forward to find hope and healing. God, please show me the way."

You can't always control what happens to you, but you can choose how you will respond.

ARE YOU READY TO GET REAL?

This is a book for people who want to follow the path to hope and healing. There's only one requirement. You have to be willing to get real: with God, with yourself, and with everyone else. I'm telling you right up front: If you like books that give THE definitive answer—neatly packaged and distilled into ten simple steps—you will not like this book. If you like books written by straight-A students who know all the answers, who never blow it, never doubt God, and never struggle, you will not like this book. Repeat: You will not like this book! But if you're willing to enroll in a class taught by a fellow student of life, I welcome you to read along. I think you should know that I've pulled no punches. The test for every sentence was "Is this true in *my own life* . . . or is this a nice platitude that 'ought' to be true? Am I just writing this because it sounds like something Christians are 'supposed to' say?" If it wasn't true *for me*, I didn't write it. As a result, this book is guaranteed to contain 0 percent *oughts* and *shoulds* and 100 percent real life.

Since I'm asking you to be honest, here's an honest confession: I've wasted years of my life arguing with God. I've expended immeasurable time and energy telling him how unfair he was, how unfair the universe was, how life had done me wrong, how everybody else got a fair shake while I got a raw deal. Nothing in my life made sense to me. I resented almost everyone on the planet because I didn't think anyone's suffering could possibly compare with mine. When I met people who had clearly suffered more, I resented them too, because they got more sympathy than me. In case you haven't guessed it by now, I was an emotional wreck.

> **This book is guaranteed to contain 0% oughts *and* shoulds *and* 100% real life.**

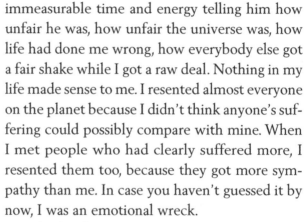

The hardest part was this: In many ways, I was absolutely right. Life had been unfair to me. I had faced some tough exams. My circumstances were incredibly painful. Significant people in my life had hurt me, and "they" were clearly wrong. I was clearly right. Guess how far "being right" got me? It wasn't until I let go of the need to be right and started pursuing the need to be healed that I found any hope for a better life.

I can say unequivocally that I am a completely different person today than I was when I set out to write this book. I don't have all the answers, and I've flunked my share of tests, but I do know one thing for sure: What God has done in my life is nothing short of miraculous. He has transformed me from "The Dead Woman Walking"[1] into a glorious testimony to the power of Christ's resurrection. I now know, with every fiber of my being, that God can bring new life where there was once nothing but death. If he can breathe life back into my weary heart, mind, and soul, there's hope for everyone.

It wasn't until I let go of the need to be right and started pursuing the need to be healed that I found any hope for a better life.

My initial goal in writing *This Isn't the Life I Signed Up For* was simply to offer comfort to women like myself who felt like they'd been mysteriously plopped down into the middle of the wrong life. I had no idea that God was going to give me answers to questions that had baffled me

for years. In fact, I had actually come to the place where I didn't believe there were any answers other than "Life is tough. Hold on till you get to heaven." I know differently now.

I know what it feels like to survey your life and conclude, "This isn't the life I signed up for!" At last I have experienced that incredible moment when I can honestly add the declaration "But I'm finding hope and healing!" God is bringing good out of the pain—much to my astonishment and delight. I am certain he can do the same for you. It is my prayer that you will find hope and healing on the pages of this book. And if you read it with an open heart and mind, I'm confident you will.

At the end of each chapter you'll find the Growth Guide, because *working* through this material, as opposed to simply *reading* through it, can make the difference between being entertained and changing your life. I hope you find this book

---

[1] Believe it or not, this was actually the nickname one of my family members gave me. That's how filled with grief and despair my life was.

thought-provoking, stimulating, convicting, and yes, entertaining. But if that's all that happens, I will have failed in my purpose. My purpose is to give you what God has given me: a chance to discover the life you did sign up for.

GROWTH GUIDE

Key Points to Remember

- No one signs up for the challenges of life, but in the real world, tough times are inevitable.
- When faced with life's heartaches, we have a choice: stay stuck in the place of pain or move forward to find hope and healing.
- God sets choices before each of us every day; every moment we are making choices that lead either to life or death.
- God could have created a world filled with flawless humans who had no choice but to do the right thing; he chose to give us free will instead.
- We are created in the image of God, and I believe he finds more joy in one person who *chooses* to love him—and to keep on loving him even in the face of tragedy—than he finds in all the beauty of every other created thing combined.
- This book is about truth, and some of it will be hard to hear. The truth will set you free, but first it's apt to hurt your feelings.
- An easy life isn't necessarily a good life, and a good life is rarely easy.
- It's time to let go of the need to be right and start pursuing the need to be healed.

Application Questions

1. Have you ever felt trapped in the middle of "the life you didn't sign up for"? Perhaps you feel that way now. Describe.

   I've always had the desire of death for myself. I want to be with God in heaven. I want to learn to live.

2. What are some of the heartaches and challenges you've faced in your life? *Molestation, rape, denial, persecution, hatred. "mental illness"*

3. In the past, have you chosen to stay stuck in the place of pain? Describe the results. *Yes, Anger. Angry at EVERYONE. I don't know why. I didn't get the "life" I envisioned. Throw my life back at God.*

4. Are you now ready to move forward to find hope and healing? If so, what has motivated you to do so at this time? *Anger   Tired of being angry. I want life.*

5. How do you typically respond when someone tells you something you didn't want to hear?

I feel attacked.

6. Recall a time in your life when the truth set you free (only after it hurt your feelings).

Stop spending money. Stop being so angry. Stop drinking.

7. In what ways have you felt life has been unfair to you? Why? *Molestation, Rape, Mental Illness.*

8. How have you responded in those times, and do you feel God was pleased with your actions?

Responded angry & child like. always wanted my way.

9. What is your definition of "getting real"?

Being CLEAN.

10. What keeps you from getting real?

Stubborn. Childish

11. What do you hope to accomplish by getting real?

Freedom—

12. What percentage of your suffering, do you think, is the natural consequences of your own choices?

99%

13. If you were to rank your lifelong level of suffering on a scale of 1 to 10, where would you be? (1 being a just-about-perfect life; 10 being ~~bankrupt,~~ quadriplegic, or sole survivor of a plane crash in the jungles of Ecuador)

10

Digging Deeper

- Read Isaiah 61:1–3:

  What does God promise to do for us in times of trials if
  we trust him?

  A day of vengeance

  What will he give us instead of ashes?

  a day of his splendor

  Why did he promise this? *Because he first loved
  us.*

  In what area of your life do you need to exchange ashes
  for beauty? *Bitterness, anger,
  hurt, sadness, pain.*

- Read 2 Kings 20:4–5:

  What does God hear and see?

  All (things)

  What does he promise to do?

  Set us FREE.

- Meditate on Psalm 139:

  What does God know about you?

  Everything

  Is he surprised by your life circumstances?

  No

  What comfort did you find in this psalm? Express your
  gratitude to God, who made you, loves you, and knows all
  the days ordained for you. *He, knows everything
  good and bad & can take
  all pain, hurt, etc. away.*

30

Look up each of the following verses and note what you discover about hope and/or healing:

Jeremiah 30:17 *God is the one who heals all wounds. Delivers.*

Jeremiah 33:6 *As above*

Luke 8:43–48 *The woman was healed*

Proverbs 12:18

Proverbs 13:17–18

Proverbs 15:4

Isaiah 58:6–9

Malachi 4:2

Psalm 25:3–7

Psalm 31:22–24

Working It Into Your Life

Make a list of the top five things you didn't sign up for. Pray over each one and ask God to show you how each one "worked together for good" by teaching you valuable life lessons.

What Happened

1. _____

2. _____

3. _____

4. _____

5. _____

Lesson Learned

1. _____

2. _____

3. _____

4. _____

5. _____

If you are completing this study as part of a small group, gather personal items or photos to represent the top five things you didn't sign up for, and be prepared to briefly describe the lesson you learned or one good thing that came out of the experience.

Review your list and ask God to show you someone who is currently facing a similar challenge. Either call or write that person a note of encouragement, sharing one Scripture God used to encourage you.

Rewrite This Week's Key Verse

_____

_____

_____

_____

_____

_____

Your Prayer in Response

_____

_____

_____

_____

_____

_____

_____

_____

_____

_____

Heavenly Father, you know this isn't the life I signed up for. There have been heartaches and disappointments along the way—some of them because of my own foolish choices. I ask you now to send the Holy Spirit to do a work of healing in my life. Fill me with hope for a better future.
In Jesus' name. Amen.

I didn't sign up for a painful childhood

CHAPTER TWO

I Didn't Sign Up for a Painful Childhood

When he lies, he speaks his native language, for he is a liar and the father of lies.

John 8:44

If you keep on biting and devouring each other, watch out or you will be destroyed by each other.

Galatians 5:15

It was Veteran's Day, and I was a guest at a small church in rural Ohio, where I had just finished leading a women's conference. The pastor invited all the veterans to stand up, state their name, branch of service, number of years served, and the military theater in which they served. By the time all of them had spoken, I was weeping uncontrollably. This might not have been a problem except that I was scheduled to deliver the morning message. I stood in front of the packed church, struggling to pull myself together, unable to utter a word for several minutes.

The wars that have shaped modern history have shaped my life too. Just looking at the gray hairs and fragile bodies of the WWII veterans was enough to shake me. They served as an undeniable reminder that my once invincible father—the tough-talking, Harley-riding man who invented cool—was no more. He had been transformed before my very eyes into the unthinkable: an old man and a daily reminder that I'm getting older too.

My father was part of the famous 101st Airborne—the Screaming Eagles who dropped out of the skies over Europe, bringing victory wherever they trod. We grew up on WWII movies, and we always imagined my father as the hero in every story. So it was only natural for my oldest brother to volunteer to serve in the Airborne when the Vietnam War rolled around. He was seventeen years old the day he signed up, dreaming of medals—like the Purple Heart my father kept in the nightstand beside his bed. The one we kids would sometimes sneak in to look at when my dad was on the road. It made us feel safe—like we had a hero to protect us.

The medal was the only part of what he signed up for that became a reality for my brother. During his first weeks in Vietnam, he watched seventy-eight of the eighty young men he'd gone through Jump School with get slaughtered in a single battle. The nightmare was just beginning. For him, for our family, for millions of Americans, the Vietnam War was a harrowing ordeal. By the time my brother had completed his tour of duty he was a heroin addict. Before long three of my brothers and one of my sisters were addicted to the drug as well. No one in my family had signed up for heroin addiction, but apparently it had signed up for us. Our whole world was turned upside down as my parents and the rest of us kids tried to make sense of the senseless—tried to retain our sanity in the midst of the insanity.

Somehow, I got lost in the middle of the mess, and it's taken me a long, long time to get found again. I can't describe what happened to me, but if you've lived through something similar, I don't need to. And if you have never found yourself in a place where *other people's choices* rocked your world, I'm not sure I can capture the powerless feeling that overtakes you.

This isn't the life I signed up for! I wanted to scream. And I did scream it, in a million different ways—none of them healthy or wise, although some were more socially acceptable than others. Because I was so ashamed of the problems in our family, I felt like "the little girl no one was allowed to play with." Rejection haunted my every step. It was almost as if I had emblazoned a sign on my forehead: "Please reject me and get it over with." Emotional pain became a way of life for me. An atmosphere. The air I breathed. The ocean I swam in. The jungle I inhabited—a land of cannibals.

HOW A CHILD GROWS UP TO BECOME A CANNIBAL

You know what a cannibal is, right? A cannibal is someone who eats other people. But do you know why cannibals eat other people? It's not for the taste. They do it because they believe the very act of consuming another human being will somehow make them more powerful. Sound familiar? I'm talking about emotional cannibalism here. I'm talking about people who feel the only way they can lift themselves up is by tearing other people down. I'm talking about self-appointed critics, people who know what's wrong with everyone except the person in the mirror. I'm talking about gossips and backbiters.

I'm talking about myself.

A cannibal is someone who eats other people.

At least that's who I used to be. I didn't sign up to become an emotional cannibal. But I became one anyway. The Scripture says this is a dangerous way to live. "If you keep on biting and devouring each other, watch out or you will be destroyed by each other" (Galatians 5:15). If only more Christians would heed that warning, the local church would be a much safer place for everyone.

THE DESTRUCTIVE SEED PLANTER

Cannibals aren't born; they're made. And nothing breeds cannibalism like a painful childhood. Just as God is the Lover of Your Soul—the One who wants to speak life and truth to your heart—you also have an enemy.[1] And I am absolutely convinced that the enemy of your soul comes early in life. In John 8:44, Jesus said, in speaking of Satan, "When he lies, he speaks his native language, for he is a liar and the father of lies." Now, what does it take to be a father? Especially in today's world, all you have to do is plant the seed and take a hike. (Of course, you may then find yourself on some television show being publicly subjected to a paternity test . . . but that's a whole different point.) I think that's exactly the kind of father Satan is. He plants his seed and takes a hike. Then the world comes along, waters it, and the seed begins to grow. The lie takes on a life of its own.

Satan isn't stupid. He knows the earlier he plants his seed, the deeper it will take root and the more difficult it will be to uproot later. He also knows that the most powerful truth in the universe is that we have a loving heavenly Father. That's why he works overtime whispering in the ears of child molesters, goading them

---

[1] When I use the term *enemy* I am not referring to Satan personally. He can only be in one place at a time, so the chances of his personally attacking you at any given moment are quite remote. Instead, I am referring to that legion of fallen angels who work to advance his agenda.

on in their filthy work. He knows our image of the Father is marred by our image of earthly fathers—or any male authority figure. Is it any wonder that some estimates show one in four American girls is sexually molested before the age of eighteen? The liar is behind it. The destructive seed planter is behind it.

Now, this is important to keep in mind: Just as God chooses to work on the earth through human beings, so does the enemy. He almost always chooses a tool—a human being through whom to sow his seed. And he always watches for an opportune moment to act. Perhaps the tool was your mother. And the moment was the day when you came home after being brutally picked on at school *again*. You had reached your limit. You needed to know for sure that you mattered to someone, that you really were a lovable human being. But no one told your mom on Thursday, October 15, 1975, at 4:00 PM that she needed to forget about making the casserole for the ladies' Bible study and focus her attention entirely on you. She didn't know this was going to be a pivotal moment in your emotional development. But the enemy knew, so he used the defective oven and a few irritating phone calls that afternoon. That's why your mom started screaming at you about socks on the floor the minute you walked through the door. That's why you were sent to your room rather than cuddled in the rocking chair.

The most powerful truth in the universe is that we have a loving heavenly Father.

You see, it wasn't about your mom. She never intended to fail you when you needed her most. Your mom wasn't your enemy. Satan, the originator of all human suffering, used his minions to orchestrate your suffering.

Maybe you're sitting there thinking, "Who is she kidding? My mother failed me every day of my life. My father completely abandoned me. It wasn't just one moment; it was every moment. My entire childhood is a painful blur." If your parents inflicted pain of that magnitude, you can be certain they did so because they were in some tremendous pain of their own. Only hurting people can systematically hurt other people. People in pain inflict the most pain on people they are supposed to love.

That doesn't justify their actions, and it doesn't diminish the damage done, but it takes away some of the sting when you realize it wasn't personal. It wasn't about you. Their actions say *nothing* about your worth as a human being. Instead, they speak volumes about the brokenness of the one(s) who failed you. I sometimes hear adults say, "My parents just didn't love me." Yet if you ask them, "Do you love your children?" they answer, "Of course I do! What a ridiculous question." Do you personally know anyone who doesn't love their children? With very few exceptions, parents love their children. Now, whether they are capable of effectively demonstrating that love is a different matter entirely. But it should come as some comfort to realize that your parents almost certainly DID love you. They just didn't always know how to show it.

THE SEED IN FULL BLOOM

As long as you continue to buy into the lie, you'll be vulnerable to the schemes of the Destructive Seed Planter. He will be able to exert a negative influence on your behavior and consequently, to a large extent, your destiny. As long as you believe the lie, you'll live like a cannibal.

In an effort to motivate you to let go of the lie, let me show you a cannibal in action and see if you recognize yourself. Let's imagine that Denise and Sue go out to lunch to talk about plans for the upcoming ladies' retreat. Now, unbeknown to Sue, Denise is secretly a cannibal, and poor unsuspecting Sue has no idea that *she is on the menu.* Sometime between the minestrone soup and the chicken Caesar salad, Denise turns to Sue and says, "I really hope you're not planning to sing again this year. I've got to be honest with you: Your solo last year really fell flat. I'm thinking my daughter could do something more upbeat and, you know, contemporary." Denise spends the remainder of the luncheon bragging on her daughter. (God help her daughter if she fails to give Denise something to brag about . . . but I'm getting ahead of myself.)

Now, Sue has a couple of options here. Option #1: Let it go. She can say to herself, "Well, that's just Denise. I know she's overcome some tough obstacles in her life. She doesn't mean to hurt people when she says stuff like that. She's just desperate to be the center of attention all the time. It's really a shame, because I know she loves God and wants to make a difference. I need to pray for her. Maybe God can use me to bring about some healing in her life."

Of course, Sue can only respond with that kind of compassion if she's dealt with her own pain. If she hasn't, she'll most likely choose Option #2. That is, she'll be furious with Denise. She'll run home, pick up the phone, and call Wendy: "You're not gonna believe what Denise just said to me. She does this stuff all the time. I can't stand her. When I hang up, I'm calling the pastor and telling him to forget about it. I'm resigning from the retreat committee."

To which Wendy responds, "That's nothing! You should hear what Denise said about Mildred. She said her grandson is a homosexual. I don't know if it's true, but you know he just moved to San Francisco. What does *that* tell you?"

Well, Sue doesn't know what to think of that, but she does know one thing. She's sick of being treated so unfairly at the First Christian Church. "I've had it with that church," she declares.

"If that's the way people want to be, then I'll just go somewhere else. And they call themselves *Christians!*"

Kind of crazy, when you think about it. Sue has just allowed someone else's low opinion of her singing talent to become the centerpiece of her existence. Tell me you've never done the same thing!

THE HEART OF THE MATTER

Now we're getting to the heart of the matter. What determines which option Sue will choose? Quite simply this: whether or not she has allowed God to uproot her own destructive seeds. Let me change the scenario just slightly, and this will become obvious to you. Let's imagine these two women back at the restaurant. Denise turns to Sue and shouts, "Oh, no!!! You have pink giraffes growing out of your ears!!!"

When we see the other person's brokenness, it's so much easier to let go of our own hurt.

Is this going to throw Sue for an emotional loop? Is she going to run home in an angry snit and start dialing for dollars? Is she going to storm the pastor's office and quit the church? No. She's going to recognize that this is not about her. It's about Denise. Denise has serious problems and needs serious prayer. When we see the other person's brokenness, it's so much easier to let go of our own hurt.

Sue will only react in anger and bitterness IF—now don't miss this part—IF Denise's words resonate with something deep inside of her. That is to say, if the destructive seed is still flourishing within her. The reason Sue flips out is because *the words ring true.* A familiar voice begins whispering in her ear: "She's right. You can't sing. You made a fool of yourself last year. You'll never be good enough. Don't ever try again." Depending on which game the enemy is playing, he might try the opposite approach: "Aha! They found you out. They all know what a phony you are! You better run. Better hide. Quick, go to another church and try harder next time."

Each lie is like a button in our heart. And every time one of those buttons gets pushed, we jump! And when we jump, we inevitably bump into other people, and when we do, someone is bound to get hurt. The more buttons you have, the more jumping you do. The more people you bump into, the more people you hurt. And since you're bumping and jumping all the time, you're hurt and exhausted in the process.

To be honest, I had so many buttons in my heart, all you had to say to me was "Donna, you look pretty today" and I'd get offended. I'd be thinking, *What? You thought I looked ugly yesterday?* Or "Donna, hey, you look like you've lost weight." My gut reaction would be *What? You thought I looked fat?* So no matter what anyone said, I took offense. I would always take it the wrong way. Of course, if you said *nothing* about my personal appearance or weight-loss efforts, I'd get offended about that too. There was just no winning with me.

RELEASE THE LIE

Now do you see the power of those childhood lies? Do you see how they can have a profound impact on your current behavior? How they can shape even the most casual interactions in your everyday life? That's why it is so incredibly important to release the lie and neutralize the power of the past. As is often said, your history doesn't have to equal your destiny.

The lie the enemy planted in my heart was pretty basic: No one wants to play with you. No one ever will. Everyone you meet will reject you. It's guaranteed. You might as well go ahead and give them a good reason to do it, so you can get it over with. It's the same basic lie he tells most kids: You're less than everyone else. You'll never measure up. You're not good enough, so don't even bother to try. Alternatively: You're not good enough, so you better try harder, try harder, try harder, until you drive yourself into a premature grave.

You didn't sign up to be lied to, but you were lied to anyway. The first step toward breaking free from the pain of your childhood is releasing the lie. Ask God, right now, to show you the lie that was planted. Then ask him to bring to your remembrance the very moment it was first planted and occasions when it was well watered. Fearlessly face the pain of those moments. Face the lie head on and see it for what it was and is: a device of the enemy.

God never reveals our pain in order to hurt us. He reveals it so he can heal it.

Once you have done that, you are ready to ask the Holy Spirit to operate: to reach in and surgically remove the lie. Realize that he may need to do some exploratory surgery in the process, and in so doing he may reveal tumors and cancerous growths that you didn't even know you had. Rather than being frightened by that, be encouraged. God never reveals our pain in order to hurt us. He reveals it so he can heal it. The fact that you didn't know about the disease doesn't mean it hasn't been silently killing you. If you are routinely angry, offended, or disappointed, I guarantee you've got a lie that needs to be uprooted.

At some point, no doubt while you are recovering from the surgery, you've got to have the following conversation with the Destructive Seed Planter.

> I'm not going to believe your lies—not one more day. I refuse to let this defeat me. I've wasted enough years allowing the pain of my childhood to control me. The people who hurt me

have no right to determine my destiny. They don't deserve that much power over my life. I'm not going to let them rent space in my head anymore. I am hereby serving them—and you—with eviction notices. Get out! And while I'm at it, I'm going to close the door on you by choosing to forgive the people who hurt me most. I know they inflicted pain because they were in pain.

YEARBOOK REALITY CHECK

Not long ago I was visiting a friend's house when she broke out her high school yearbook and insisted I take a look. Truth be told, I had no desire to look at her yearbook. For me, high school was a painful place filled with intimidating characters—big, frightening giants. Imagine my surprise when I began leafing through the pages and saw a bunch of hapless teenagers. Gradually it occurred to me: *Her yearbook looks exactly like mine. This could be my high school. All the same cast of characters, the same cliques, even the same hairstyles, and no doubt the same insecurities.*

It was one of those rare moments when I stopped being the only person in the world who had to endure life's little indignities. I felt tenderness in my heart for every teenager in America—and every one of my fellow humans who had survived the journey and gone on to adulthood. As we realize that we're not alone, that everyone has a story to tell, it brings our own life into perspective.

Perspective is a beautiful thing.

GROWTH GUIDE

Key Points to Remember

- Sometimes other people's choices rock our world, because we must reap the consequences of their poor choices. That can leave us feeling powerless.

- The sense of powerlessness can lead us to become emotional cannibals.
- An emotional cannibal is someone who tries to make herself feel more powerful by consuming (or as the Scripture says, "devouring") other people.
- Satan acts as the Destructive Seed Planter, planting lies deep in our hearts, and he usually comes early to do his dirty work.
- Just as God works through people to accomplish his purposes on the earth, so Satan works through human vessels to plant his destructive lies.
- Each lie planted in your heart is like a hot button—when people push it, you jump!
- If you are routinely angry, offended, or disappointed, you've got lies that need to be uprooted.
- Other people's actions toward you say nothing about your worth as a human being. Instead, they speak volumes about the brokenness of the one(s) who failed you.

Application Questions

1. What are some of the events that have shaped your life (in particular, in your childhood)?

2. What are some of the ways you have screamed to be heard in your life?

3. Are you an emotional cannibal?

4. Can you think of some occasions when you've tried to make yourself feel more powerful by consuming someone else?

5. Have you ever been the victim of emotional cannibalism?

6. What were the results in your life?

7. Have you seen the destructive influence of emotional cannibals in your church? What have been the results?

8. Could you identify with the cannibal at lunch scenario? If you were in that scene, which role would you be more likely to fall into? The cannibal, or the woman "on the menu"?

9. How hard is it for you to let it go when someone hurts your feelings?

10. How likely are you to start "dialing for dollars" and working yourself into an angry snit over some offense?

11. Have you ever allowed someone else's opinion of you to become the centerpiece of your existence?

12. What were some of the destructive lies planted in your heart?

13. Do you know who planted them?

14. What has been the result of believing those lies?

15. What lies have YOU unwittingly planted in the lives of your own children?

16. What steps do you need to take to undo the damage done?

Digging Deeper

- Read Matthew 15:16–19:

  What sins does Jesus specifically mention?

  Were you surprised to find *slander* listed among the other sins we might consider far more serious?

  How does that make you feel about your involvement with slander?

  Look up *slander* in the dictionary. Write the definition below.

  Have you been guilty of slandering someone? Who?

  What steps do you need to take to make things right?

- Read 1 Peter 5:6–10:

  What two character qualities are mentioned in verse 8?

  How can these prepare us to stand firm in the face of attacks?

  How should we respond when the devil tries to devour us (perhaps sending a human vessel to do the job)?

- Read Psalm 27:10:
  Who does this passage say may forsake you?

  What does the inclusion of this passage imply about the relationship between some parents and their children?

  Who does this passage assure us will never forsake us?

- Meditate on Psalm 86:
  Who does the psalmist want to "hear" him?

  Do you tell your problems to God, or to everyone else?

  What does the psalmist ask God to do for him?

  List some of God's character qualities mentioned in the psalm.

  How can knowing who God is help you recover from the pain/power of destructive seeds?

It is not enough to uproot lies. We have to replace them with the truth. Be sure to fill your mind with God's truth and his promises that apply to your specific area of need so that the vacancy left by uprooted lies can be filled with truth rather than a new set of lies. Look up the following passages and note what truths you discover about your identity and the basis of your security:

Deuteronomy 33:12

Isaiah 43:4

Isaiah 49:16

Isaiah 54:9–10

Romans 8:14–17

Romans 8:38–39

1 Thessalonians 1:4

Ephesians 4:24

1 Peter 2:9–10

1 John 3:1

Working It Into Your Life

List five lies that were planted in your heart, along with the person who planted them. If you are concerned about confidentiality, you can write your answer on a separate piece of paper and destroy it after your surgery.

Lie   Seed Planter

1._____   1._____

2._____   2._____

3._____   3._____

4._____   4._____

5._____   5._____

Set aside time for the Holy Spirit to uproot those lies. Pray and grieve over each one. You might adapt the following declaration:

> I'm not going to believe destructive lies—not one more day. I refuse to let them defeat me. I've wasted enough years allowing the pain of my childhood to control me. The people who hurt me have no right to determine my destiny. They don't deserve that much power over my life. I'm not going to let them rent space in my head anymore. I am hereby serving them—and the enemy—with eviction notices. *Get out!* And while I'm at it, I'm going to close the door to the enemy by choosing to

forgive the people who hurt me most. I know they inflicted pain because they were in pain.

Now ask God to show you the brokenness of each seed planter. Take out photos of those people if you have them available and seek to see each person through God's eyes.

Seed Planter	Source of His/Her Brokenness
1. _____	1. _____
2. _____	2. _____
3. _____	3. _____
4. _____	4. _____
5. _____	5. _____

If you can find the strength to do so, you will find it incredibly healing to actually pray for the ones who have caused you pain. You might pray specifically that God will help them overcome the source of their brokenness and the lies that were planted in their hearts. I know, from personal experience, how hard this is. I also know, ultimately, how healing it is.

If you are part of a small group, bring photos from your childhood and your yearbook (or other symbols of the seed planters in your life) with you to class.

Rewrite One of This Week's Key Verses

_____

_____

_____

_____

_____

_____

Your Prayer in Response

_____

_____

_____

_____

_____

_____

_____

_____

_____

_____

Heavenly Father, thank you for sending your Holy Spirit to lead me into all truth. I thank you for the words of your Son, Jesus, that tell me I WILL know the truth and it WILL set me free. Help me to break free from the power of lies and begin to walk in the power of truth. Help me to forgive others, just as you, through Christ, forgave me. Amen.

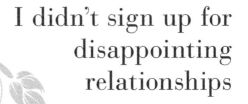

I didn't sign up for
disappointing
relationships

CHAPTER THREE

I Didn't Sign Up for Disappointing Relationships

See to it that no one misses the grace of God and that no bitter root grows up to cause trouble and defile many.

Hebrews 12:15

In chapter 2, we discovered that just as God works through human vessels to accomplish his purposes on the earth, so does the enemy. As I've ministered to women around the world, it has become increasingly obvious that the area of greatest heartache is disappointing relationships. No one walks down the aisle thinking, *Hmm, I hope this man makes me miserable for the rest of my life.* No one reaches out in friendship to another person thinking, *I'm looking forward to the day when this person totally betrays me.* No one signs up for disappointing relationships. But in the real world, we all have them. If we're honest, we also have the pain of knowing we have been a disappointment to others.

FORGIVENESS, THE TOOL

Because we are all only jars of clay, it's inevitable that we will disappoint one another on a fairly routine basis. In fact, just last Friday night I had to pull my twelve-year-old daughter aside and say, "Listen, I know you are disappointed in Mommy right now, and I'm so sad about that. I promise you I'm going to try harder. I hope you'll be able to forgive me." If you haven't had a similar conversation with one of your children recently, you're probably overdue.

I firmly believe the power to forgive is the most powerful tool—and the most precious gift—God has given us. I wonder why we don't use it more often. When we seek forgiveness, we make ourselves vulnerable. We acknowledge our frailty and ask for another chance. When we extend forgiveness, I believe we are closer to the heart of God than at any other time. Colossians 3:13 says, "Bear with each other and forgive whatever grievances you may have against one another. Forgive as the Lord forgave you."

The more forgiving and gracious we are to others, the more they will be willing to extend forgiveness and grace to us.

How did the Lord forgive us? Unconditionally. When did the Lord forgive us? When we least deserved it. I'm finding that the universe makes more and more sense as I apply the fundamental realization that nine times out of ten, we get what we give. This is even true in the area of forgiveness: "Forgive, and you will be forgiven" (Luke 6:37). The more forgiving and gracious we are to others, the more they will be willing to extend forgiveness and grace to us. As we become increasingly willing to give others the benefit of the doubt, others will do the same for us. Very few people are genuinely malicious or out to get you. And those who are, need a Savior, not your condemnation or anger. Look how Jesus responded to the people who crucified him: "Jesus said, 'Father, forgive them, for they do not know what they are doing' " (Luke 23:34).

He gave them the benefit of the doubt to the nth degree, wouldn't you say? As you spend time in prayer, seeking God's perspective on your disappointing relationships, God will give you the same revelation in a very personal way. Eventually you will come to that glorious place of freedom when you release the pain and cry out, "Father, forgive _____, for he did not know what he was doing."

IS THERE AN *IF* IN FORGIVENESS?

God takes the matter of forgiveness very seriously: "For if you forgive men when they sin against you, your heavenly Father will also forgive you. But if you do not forgive men their sins, your Father will not forgive your sins" (Matthew 6:14–15).

I don't know about you, but I find the word *if* in the above verses rather frightening! In fact, my kids and I refer to these as the scariest verses in the Bible. I find it difficult to reconcile this passage with the foundation of my theology, which says, "If you confess with your mouth, 'Jesus is Lord,' and believe in your heart that God raised him from the dead, you will be saved" (Romans 10:9). I mean, you pray the prayer and you're good to go, right? Still, the *if* remains, and frankly, I'm not sure what to do with it. Here's what I've told my daughters (if you have a better explanation, please e-mail me):

If we are unwilling to forgive others, then we haven't really understood what the cross means. We haven't really understood the price Jesus paid for our sins—and how can we truly believe when we don't even understand? Consider the following passage from Matthew 18, the parable of the unforgiving debtor:

Then Peter came to Jesus and asked, "Lord, how many times shall I forgive my brother when he sins against me? Up to seven times?"

Jesus answered, "I tell you, not seven times, but seventy-seven times.

"Therefore, the kingdom of heaven is like a king who wanted to settle accounts with his servants. As he began the settlement, a man who owed him ten thousand talents was brought to him. Since he was not able to pay, the master ordered that he and his wife and his children and all that he had be sold to repay the debt.

"The servant fell on his knees before him. 'Be patient with me,' he begged, 'and I will pay back everything.' The servant's master took pity on him, canceled the debt and let him go.

"But when that servant went out, he found one of his fellow servants who owed him a hundred denarii. He grabbed him and began to choke him. 'Pay back what you owe me!' he demanded.

"His fellow servant fell to his knees and begged him, 'Be patient with me, and I will pay you back.'

"But he refused. Instead, he went off and had the man thrown into prison until he could pay the debt. When the other servants saw what had happened, they were greatly distressed and went and told their master everything that had happened.

"Then the master called the servant in. 'You wicked servant,' he said, 'I canceled all that debt of yours because you begged me to. Shouldn't you have had mercy on your fellow servant just as I had on you?' In anger his master turned him over to the jailers to be tortured, until he should pay back all he owed.

"This is how my heavenly Father will treat each of you unless you forgive your brother from your heart" (Matthew 18:21–35).

UNFORGIVENESS AND THE SCHEMES OF THE ENEMY

When we truly understand what God has done for us, forgiving others will become second nature. In the following passage, Paul is warning a local church against holding grudges, due to the destructive power of unforgiveness:

> If you forgive anyone, I also forgive him. And what I have forgiven—if there was anything to forgive—I have forgiven in the sight of Christ for your sake, in order that Satan might not outwit us. For we are not unaware of his schemes. (2 Corinthians 2:10–11)

You may be thinking, *What does forgiveness have to do with Satan and his schemes?* EVERYTHING! He knows the power of forgiveness better than anyone. It was God's willingness to provide a means of forgiveness for the human race that foiled Satan's plans at the cross. What is Satan's scheme in your life? It's real simple. To keep you stuck in your old ways. To keep you so focused on who did what, and who said what, and how dare they, and you've had it, etc., that you can't move forward with the rest of your life. Trust me on this one. I know from personal experience.

I'll never forget meeting a woman at one of my conferences. She had tears in her eyes as she told me she had gone through a painful divorce. I reached out my hand to comfort her. Her whole body was trembling with hurt. Her words were filled with resentment; her tone of voice dripped with bitterness. I assumed the wound was fresh. However, as her story began to unfold, I realized this was not a recent occurrence. When I asked her how long she had been divorced, she replied, "Twenty-two years." I just about fell on the floor!

What a victory for the enemy. No wonder this woman's entire

family lived in upheaval. No wonder her health was a wreck. She may not have signed up for a disappointing relationship; she certainly didn't sign up for divorce; but until she forgives her ex-husband, she is signing up DAILY to let the enemy have a field day with her life.

I want to come back to where we left off in the last chapter. Do you remember we asked the Holy Spirit to uproot the lie planted in your heart by the Destructive Seed Planter? We can't leave things there! Once you have asked the Holy Spirit to uproot the lie, it will probably be painfully obvious who Satan used to plant it there in the first place. You might also recognize a variety of seed-waterers who were used to reinforce the lie. The temptation is to let those revelations make you bitter, although chances are you are already filled with bitterness toward them, even if it's only on a subconscious level. As a little aside: Do you have a person or persons in your life to whom you invariably speak in a certain tone of voice? Even when they haven't done anything offensive at that particular moment? That's your cue to look for deep-seated bitterness that needs to be dealt with.

You should take these revelations as your invitation to forgive the person or people involved. Realize they were merely pawns in a cruel game. In their own way, they were most certainly victims before they became victimizers.

OVERCOMING RESENTMENT

My daughter Leah had been hurt—devastated, actually—by the behavior of someone she loved very much. As a result, I could see that a root of bitterness and resentment was beginning to grow. Hebrews 12:15 warns us: "See to it that no one misses the grace of God and that no bitter root grows up to cause trouble and defile many." Bitterness is like a contagious disease: first it spreads throughout our own body; then it begins to overtake the people around us.

One night as we sat talking, God led me to share with her a quote from Henri Nouwen:

> One way for me to deal with my resentment is to acknowledge the suffering of the other person. Whenever I'm hurt, I perceive the other person as strong, and myself as weak. But when I'm willing to consider the other person's individual history with struggle and agony, I can prevent myself from judging too harshly or making a final angry statement about their behavior.[1]

Bitterness is like a contagious disease: first it spreads throughout our own body; then it begins to overtake the people around us.

Rather than focusing on how this person had disappointed her and the pain this person had inflicted (and isn't it always a temptation to retell and rehash old hurts?), we talked about the pain the person had endured. It didn't excuse her actions, but it did explain the other person's actions. An article I read recently put it this way:

> Significant acts of forgiveness entail letting go of a precious story we tell about ourselves, risking the awareness of a larger, less self-justifying truth. . . . Owning up means getting past one's defensiveness. It means stepping out of the Blaming System, in which one person has to be not only wrong but also the bad one.[2]

---

[1] Henri Nouwen, *In the House of the Lord: The Journey From Fear to Love* (UK: Darton Longman and Todd Publishers, 1986), 15.

[2] Robert Karen, O magazine, February 2001.

AGONIZING FORGIVENESS

One danger with forgiveness, which is prevalent in the church, is something I would call "rushed forgiveness" or "sweep-it-under-the-carpet forgiveness." Sometimes well-meaning people, who don't want to face life's more painful realities, want to use forgiveness like a magic wand. They think it can make all the pain disappear and wipe out logical consequences.

My friend Martha faced this when she went through a personal crisis several years ago. She discovered that her husband had been conducting a five-year affair with a teenage girl. She vividly remembers trying to tell her pastor what was going on, but he literally put his hand up and said, "I don't need to hear intimate details." He didn't want to face it. It was too horrible, so he wanted her to sweep it under the carpet. His remedy was "Just forgive and forget about the whole thing," with the subtext being "I really don't want to face the truth that families who sit in my congregation with smiles on their faces could be living through the hell you are about to describe. If I allow myself to hear this, I will lose my plausible deniability. You'll rob me of the right to pretend this stuff can't possibly happen in Christian homes. And I don't think I can survive that. So please shut up and go away. You're scaring me."

That's not forgiveness; that's denial.

There can be no authentic forgiveness as long as we are in denial. I think it's extremely significant that the parable of the unforgiving debtor lists EXACTLY what the debt owed was, down to a fraction of a penny. That is so key! Until we confront the true cost, until we come face-to-face with what has been stolen from us and how we have been forced to pay a heavy price for the sins of others, I don't think there can be true forgiveness. When Jesus pondered the cross—when he considered paying the price for our sins—he carefully counted the cost. Indeed, the Scripture tells us:

"And being in anguish, he prayed more earnestly, and his sweat was like drops of blood falling to the ground" (Luke 22:44).

That's what I call agonizing forgiveness. It doesn't run and hide. It doesn't bury an offense or pretend it didn't matter. It looks the pain straight in the eye and says, "You hurt me so bad you nearly killed me, but because Christ died for me, his love compels me to forgive you." Nothing short of *that* type of forgiveness will ever change your life.

A HIGHER COURT

You can sweep sin under the carpet in an instant, but I believe "agonizing forgiveness" often requires a process and it may unfold over the course of time. The only One who was capable of forgiving once for all was Jesus. The rest of us have to work on it every day. For me personally, forgiving the one who hurt me most has been a long, slow journey. Just when I think I've finished the work, the Lord will show me something else I need to deal with. Now, what I'm about to share doesn't mean we should endlessly rehash old wounds and hurts. However, we do have to face facts. At one point, God actually led me to make a list detailing exactly what this person's sin had cost me. It brought me as close to sweating drops of blood as I have ever come in my entire life. I cried day and night for weeks. At one point, my daughter asked me if I thought I would ever stop crying. I told her I didn't know for sure. And I honestly didn't.

> *"Agonizing forgiveness" often requires a process and it may unfold over the course of time.*

God forced me to confront the full truth. And just when the pain was about to overwhelm me, God said, "Now give me the list." I felt like the Lord gave me a word picture at that time. I was sitting in a courtroom with my list. I was the plaintiff, the prosecuting attorney, and the judge all rolled into one. I was forcefully presenting my case and passing judgments left and right. The Lord stepped into the courtroom and said, "As long as you are still trying this case—as long as it's tied up in the lower court—it will never pass to a Higher Court."

Instantly I understood. I needed to let go of this person so God could deal with him. *Perfect*, I thought, *God can dish out the punishment his sins deserve and will do a much better job of it than I can.* For a moment I was overjoyed. But then I heard God say, "What if my judgment is to grant him the same forgiveness you were granted at the foot of the cross?"

"No, Lord!" I cried. "No. Please. Don't! I want you to punish him. I want you to vindicate me before the whole world by publicly condemning him. I want you to *make him pay* for what he's done to me."

"Then you haven't really forgiven him, have you?" came the reply.

Apparently not.

I'm still working on it.

No doubt significant people in your life have disappointed you—some in small ways, others profoundly so. You didn't sign up for disappointing relationships, but they signed up for you. Now the question remains: What will you do? Will you live your life consumed by the bitterness? Will you sweep the pain under the carpet? Or will you work through the process of agonizing forgiveness until you finally reach that place where you entrust yourself entirely to him who judges justly? (1 Peter 2:23). If you are willing to cooperate with God, he is able to heal the hurt, and in so doing, you'll be well on your way to discovering the life you signed up for—a life where old hurts are left behind to make room for new joys.

GROWTH GUIDE

Key Points to Remember

- Just as God works through human vessels to accomplish his purposes on the earth, so does the enemy.
- Because we are all fragile jars of clay, it's inevitable that we will disappoint one another on a routine basis.
- Forgiveness is the most precious gift—and the most powerful tool—God has given us.
- When we extend forgiveness, we are closer to the heart of God than at any other time.
- The more gracious we are the more inclined people are to be gracious toward us.
- No one signs up to be "wronged," but until we forgive those who hurt us, we are signing up daily to let the enemy have a field day with our lives.
- Those who hurt you were most certainly victims before they became victimizers.
- Bitterness is like a contagious disease: first it spreads throughout our own body; then it begins to overtake the people around us.
- One way to deal with resentment is to acknowledge the suffering of the other person.
- Forgiveness involves "letting go of a precious story we tell about ourselves, risking the awareness of a larger, less self-justifying truth."

Application Questions

1. Recall some of the disappointing relationships in your life. Why were they a disappointment?

2. In what way did you set yourself up for disappointment by having unrealistic expectations?

3. Recall a time when you were a disappointment to others. Why did it happen?

4. How would you handle the situation differently if you had it to do all over again?

5. Do you consider yourself a forgiving—or unforgiving—person?

6. To test yourself: Are people quick to forgive you? If not, is it possible the reason is that *you* are not a forgiving person?

7. Recall the woman who had been divorced twenty-two years but was still trapped in the pain. Then as you consider the condition of your health and your family, is there any possibility that your own unforgiveness is part of the problem?

8. Is there a person in your life to whom you invariably speak in a certain tone of voice?

9. What deep-seated bitterness might be causing your negative attitude?

10. One way to deal with resentment is to acknowledge the suffering of the other person. In detail, in writing, acknowledge the pain of each person who has hurt you. (Walk a mile in their shoes.)

11. Has anyone ever pressured you to "sweep it under the carpet" rather than letting you deal with your pain?

12. What was the result?

13. As you think of the person who has hurt you most, what is your response to the following question: What if God's judgment is to grant that person the same forgiveness you were granted at the foot of the cross?

Digging Deeper

- Read Genesis 50:15–21:

  Why do you think Joseph wept when he received the message from his brothers?

  What is the significance of Joseph's rhetorical question in verse 19?

  How can you apply his perspective in verse 20 to your daily experience?

- Meditate on Psalm 25:

  In what ways can the pain of your past be likened unto "enemies"?

  Who will never be put to shame?

  What does the psalmist ask God to show him?

  What does the psalmist ask God to do for him?

  What does the psalmist reveal about who God is and what he does?

Studying the following passages, what do you learn about resentment and forgiveness?

Ephesians 4:31–32

Matthew 18:21–35

Mark 11:25

Colossians 3:12–14

Hebrews 12:14–15

2 Corinthians 2:6–11

James 3:2

Romans 2:1–4

Working It Into Your Life

1. Relationship survey: On a scale of 1 to 10, rate your contentment with each of the following relationships (1 being extremely disappointed and 10 being blissfully happy):

   _____ parents   _____ siblings
   _____ spouse   _____ children
   _____ co-workers   _____ neighbors
   _____ old friends   _____ new friends
   _____ acquaintances

   Now go back and evaluate how you might overcome disappointment in each of these relationships, and ask God to show you if part of the problem is your own unrealistic expectations. You might also write out a description of realistic expectations for each relationship.

2. Reread the description of the courtroom scene. Ask God to show you (although you probably already know) which person in your life you are most in need of forgiving. On a separate sheet of paper, make a list detailing exactly what that person has done and what his or her sin has cost you (e.g., lost opportunities for other relationships, inability to trust, physical ailments rooted in emotional turmoil, lost sleep, broken friendships).

   Now walk into the courtroom and begin advocating your case. In your own mind, picture God stepping into the courtroom and yourself giving God the list.

   Next, rewrite as many times as you need to: "Father, forgive _____, for he (or she) did not know what he (or she) was doing."

Rewrite One of This Week's Key Verses

_____

_____

_____

_____

_____

_____

Your Prayer in Response

_____

_____

_____

_____

_____

_____

_____

_____

_____

_____

Heavenly Father, thank you for the incredible gift of forgiveness. I know it is the road that led me back to your house because Jesus paved the way. Now let me experience forgiveness as the road to healing, as I forgive those who have sinned against me. Holy Spirit, lead me into the full truth about those who have hurt me. Give me new eyes to see them not as those who have hurt me but as people who have been broken by the world. In Jesus' name. Amen.

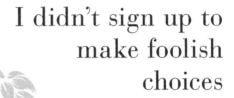

I didn't sign up to
make foolish
choices

CHAPTER FOUR

I Didn't Sign Up to Make Foolish Choices

Do not judge, or you too will be judged. For in the same way
you judge others, you will be judged, and with the measure
you use, it will be measured to you.

Matthew 7:1–2

My house was absolutely freezing. One night it was so cold in
my bedroom, my body hurt from shivering. I kept putting more
pellets into our wood-burning stove and turning it higher and
higher. I even turned up the electric heater, which I normally only
use as a backup system. But no matter how high I turned the
pellet stove, no matter how high I turned the electric thermostat,
it was still freezing in the house, especially upstairs. I thought,
There must be something wrong with the ventilation system. I went
throughout the house, carefully checking each of the heat vents

to make sure they were, indeed, spitting out hot air. All seemed to be in good working order.

Maybe I need to have the pellet stove cleaned out; maybe it's clogged or something, I thought. So I had someone come and clean out the pellet stove.

I need to add insulation to the windows, I thought. I'd seen those ads on TV where you put plastic over the windows and then blow-dry it. *Yeah, something like that might do the trick.*

I was wracking my brain trying to come up with solutions, but nothing seemed to work. I was completely baffled. This went on for several days. Finally, I identified the coldest room. Then honed in on the coldest location. I lifted up the blinds and *voila!* An open window.

I let out a scream: "TAAAAAAARRRRRRAAAAAAAA!"

That's Tara, by the way—my five-year-old. She came running into the room. I had now gathered my wits about me. "You wouldn't happen to know anything about this open window, would you?"

She knew she was in big trouble. "I wanted to watch the worker man," she said sheepishly. Let me tell you, that little girl got the lecture of a lifetime about opening windows in winter, electric bills, money not growing on trees, ingratitude, etc., etc., etc.

A couple of weeks later, I noticed that my house was really cold again. *Well, the weather is intensifying. We're on the side of a mountain; it's like a giant wind tunnel. Four walls can only keep the cold out to some degree. Better turn up that pellet stove. I'm needing to rely on that backup electric heater a lot more than I did last year.*

Do I scare you?

Anyway, this whole *Wow, it's so much colder than last year* internal monologue went on for a couple of days until I finally had an epiphany: *Donna, why don't you check Tara's window?*

DUH!

Guess what? Tara had opened another window!

Now, I'm not saying it was God's idea for Tara to disobey me after I had given her such clear directives against opening windows. But let me tell you, God sure used it to get my attention. And I do believe he sent me the message twice because he was determined I not miss it.

So what's the message? Here goes.

I had known for many years that there was something seriously wrong in my spiritual life. There were significant areas of sin that seemed absolutely entrenched, unconquerable. No matter how hard I tried to turn up the heat through attending a weekly women's Bible study and having a personal devotional time, I could not seem to move forward. Even days spent in prayer and fasting left me feeling out in the cold.

I kept thinking there must be something wrong with the heating system. Or that I needed to turn the heat higher and higher with more prayer, more Bible reading, and more study. Through Tara and the open windows, God showed me—in a very vivid way—that even though there was nothing wrong with my heating system, I could still be left out in the cold if I didn't do something about the open windows in my life. Those open windows were my judgmental attitude and my unwillingness to forgive those who had hurt me.

BAFFLING ARRAY OF TESTS

Throughout my Christian life, I've always been baffled by the fact that I seem to face a lot more tests than other people do. I thought God was picking on me. Or that the universe was just this terribly unjust, confusing place. Or alternatively, I flattered myself that God was "allowing" all these tests because:

- I was a spiritual giant and he knew that I could handle them all.
- He was using all of these experiences to mold my character so that I could be a shining beacon of godliness in a lost world.
- I was a spiritual giant, so Satan was unfairly targeting me for attack.

Sometimes God does allow "the testing of our faith," as it says in James 1:2–4:

> Consider it pure joy, my brothers, whenever you face trials of many kinds, because you know that the testing of your faith develops perseverance. Perseverance must finish its work so that you may be mature and complete, not lacking anything.

But when I looked at my own life, I had to conclude that something else was going on. The fact of the matter was, I was not a spiritual giant. I was a wreck. These experiences were not molding my character; they were warping my character. I'll say more about the fairness or unfairness of the enemy's attacks in the next chapter. I think we've got enough to deal with already.

SO MANY JUDGMENTS

One day God gave me a little revelation. "The reason you have so many tests is because you pass so many judgments!" I began pondering this idea. I should probably confess that I used to be one of those delightful people who knew exactly what was wrong with everyone and everything. You see, I had the gift of discernment. I would spend hours, literally, delivering silent sermons to everyone who had done me wrong. I pronounced judgments like a soda machine spits out cans: routinely, easily, and thoughtlessly. Yet the Scripture specifically states: "Do not judge, or you too will be judged. For in the same way you judge others, you will be judged, and with the measure you use, it will be measured to you" (Matthew 7:1–2).

God is never glad for our sin or its consequences.

God has set up the spiritual realm in such a way that you get what you give. It's called reaping what you sow, and it's one of the most powerful realities in the universe. I wasn't getting what God wanted to give me; I was just getting back what I was giving the world. So while it was true enough that a sovereign God "allowed" me

to reap the logical consequences of my sin, that's a completely different mindset than "God is allowing this trial" as in it was his idea somehow. God is never glad for our sin or its consequences. He specifically commands us, "Do NOT" do these things. And he warns us in advance what will happen when we violate these fundamental principles of the universe.

DOES GOD REALLY MEAN THAT?

I had always dismissed these verses, just like I conveniently dismissed any other verse that didn't fit in with my existing theology or mindset. I can actually remember explaining them away: "Well, this can't mean what it looks like it means. Because I know Jesus already forgave all my sin, so I am not under judgment. This must apply to all those terrible non-Christians who pick on me at work just because I'm a self-consumed, insecure lunatic. But hey, I'm forgiven and they're not. So ha-ha! Oops. Gotta hurry up and get to Bible study now. Too bad Kathy never shuts up. Bob is leading tonight. He is so clueless. The group would be waaay better if they let me lead it. I guess they're just jealous of my superior biblical insight."

Really makes you want to come play with me, huh?

I got an early jump on judging the world. It started with my family. Unfortunately, I thought I was so much better than all of them, I could hardly stand living in the same house. Clearly, I had been switched at birth. I blamed my brothers and my sister for ruining my life. They weren't the siblings I signed up for. I signed up for the Brady Bunch. For Greg and Marcia (whose worst crisis was a pimple on her forehead). I signed up for family problems that could be resolved in thirty minutes—less time out for commercials. My siblings didn't measure up, so I judged them. That was my first seriously bad move.

I didn't understand what I understand now. When we judge another human being, we set in motion some powerful spiritual forces. It's like whistling for the devil. It's like inviting him to bring on the test; to tempt us with the same stuff we judged another person for being unable to withstand. I was a freshman in high school when the enemy showed up and said, "So, you'd never be a drug addict like your brothers and sister? You're better than they are, huh? Let's just see about that."

I took the test and flunked. I never signed up to become a drug addict, but I became one anyway.

Perhaps the group I judged most harshly were divorced Christians. What a disgrace to the cause of Christ! They should be ashamed of themselves, tearing their children apart and single-handedly destroying the fabric of American society. How dare they show their faces in church ever again! I mean, how superficial can you be? Okay, so your husband had a little affair. Big deal!

Get over it! I mean, you didn't see ME getting divorced, and I can personally guarantee that my marriage was ten times worse than all other bad marriages in the history of unholy matrimony combined.

I think you know where *that* took me.

But I didn't "get it" back then, so I was blindsided when the test came. When my marriage ended in divorce, all the judgments I had passed came raining down on my head. Then I experienced firsthand the excruciating pain of rejection and condemnation of fellow believers. But God is a redeemer. And it was this very experience that God finally used to get through my thick skull. *"Donna, you want to scream from the highest mountain, 'You don't know what he's done to me! You have no idea what I've lived through.' That's exactly how all the women you judged felt. You have no idea why people do half the things they do. And it's none of your business anyway. It's my business. Your business is to love people unconditionally. You have no other assignment."*

BACK TO THE BEGINNING

So what does all this have to do with making foolish choices? Bear with me for another paragraph or so. We're getting there. You see, I wish I had known these truths as a new believer. My Christian walk would have been an entirely different experience. Let me take you back to the beginning and you can witness firsthand where I went wrong.

My life took a dramatic turn for the better when a friend invited me to take a free vacation in the mountains of northern Pennsylvania. Nothing could have fully prepared me for my trip to Tuscarora, a Lutheran Brethren retreat center. Actually, a group of Presbyterians were hosting the event I attended, and

I often joke that "nothing in the Westminster Shorter Catechism could have prepared them for the likes of me!" Somewhere around the third day, I was sitting along the Delaware River, when suddenly I understood: God had made a way for me to get a second chance at life. When Jesus came to earth two thousand years ago, he came so that we could have life. He died so that we could live. He took the punishment we deserved so that we wouldn't have to face it on our own. God was offering me a free gift; all I had to do was accept it. So I accepted it with all my heart.

And let me tell you, the day I signed up to follow Jesus, I signed up to change the world. In fact, the night after I became a Christian, I was walking alone under a beautiful moonlit sky when I heard God speak to me so clearly it was as if he were walking beside me. He said, "Donna, I'm going to take you to retreat centers just like this one all over the country, and I'm going to use you in a mighty way in my kingdom."

I couldn't believe it! The God of the universe had *picked me.* I had always felt like the last person anyone would ever pick. Maybe you were like me: You can remember dreading PE class and the whole "dividing into teams" drill. I was almost always one of the last kids picked. It went something like this:

"We're not gonna take her; you take her."

"No, we're not gonna take her."

"Tell you what. We'll give you Donna and a ten-point lead."

"Forget it."

"We'll give you Donna, a ten-point lead, and the new aluminum bat."

I know what it feels like not to be picked. Maybe you do too. So I was thrilled beyond belief to know that the God of the universe had picked me. John 15:16 says, "You did not choose me, but I chose you. . . . *to sit in the pew and take notes concerning what's wrong with everyone at your church.*" Being a zealous new believer, I set right to work on the assignment. I only recently discovered that I had misread the verse. Actually, it says, "You did not choose me, but I chose you and appointed you to go and bear fruit—fruit that will last. Then the Father will give you whatever you ask in my name."

It gets even worse. The *very next* verse reads, "This is my command: Love each other" (John 15:17).

HOW I BLEW IT BIG-TIME

Well, back in the beginning—you know, back when I knew so much—I wasn't real concerned about loving people. I was out to change the world, unlike the lightweight, superficial Christians surrounding me. I'd been a Christian for a few weeks, so I thought I had a better grasp on Christianity than *they* did. I had waited a long time to get picked for something and I wasn't gonna blow it. Except I *did* blow it.

Many of you already know my testimony, but for those who don't, I'll recap briefly. Shortly after becoming a Christian, I went off to college. The very first week, I met a young Middle Eastern Muslim man who dramatically changed the course of my life. Although I knew God specifically said, "Do not be yoked together with unbelievers" (2 Corinthians 6:14), I chose to become entangled with him anyway. Even though everyone around me pointed out my disobedience, I had started down the path and couldn't find a way to turn back. We married in 1982, and for the next eighteen years he exerted an extraordinary degree of control over my life. Even though he converted to Christianity, his cultural roots ran deep. As is customary in many Middle Eastern countries, I was not permitted to leave the house without his permission and strict supervision. To him, this was perfectly logical. He was protecting me because he loved me so much. Why would any decent woman want to go somewhere without her husband? What was I trying to hide? If I wasn't planning to do anything wrong, why should I object to his keeping constant watch over my every move?

It was absolutely maddening—but my husband couldn't figure out why I was going nuts. I remember one day in particular, I wanted to go for a walk around the block by myself—something I had always been strictly forbidden to do. So I asked my husband's permission—but his answer was no. I asked, "Can I at least sit on the front steps?" The answer again was no. As you can imagine, it's pretty tough to travel to retreat centers around the country when you're not allowed to sit alone on the front steps.

It is never God's will for us to be disobedient.

I didn't sign up to make foolish choices, but I had made a colossal one. So often we want to blame God for our predicament. Or we offer the excuse, "Well, God is in control, so it must be God's will." No, it is never God's will for us to be disobedient. My life was NOT where God wanted it to be; it was where my own foolish choices had taken me.

Is it possible you need to make some painful admissions about your own life?

IRREVOCABLE MISTAKES?

If my story ended there, this would be a seriously depressing book. Praise God, he is moving me forward to find hope and healing. I was so afraid my mistakes were irreversible. But God reassured me from his Word: "God's gifts and his call are irrevocable" (Romans 11:29). God is bigger than our mistakes.

But. Here's the big but. But at some point, we have to truly repent. We have to stop blaming God and agree with God. We have to turn around and change directions. That's what real repentance means. It's not enough to feel sorry. We have to change the way we're living.

"This isn't the life I signed up for," but when I'm completely honest, it's pretty much the logical outcome of my life choices . . . and the choices of those around me. That's not always the case. Sometimes life throws people a genuine curve ball. Something absolutely out of our control, like a child born with birth defects. I'll say more about that later, but this is the chapter on foolish mistakes. I know for me personally, there weren't any curve balls. Just my own stupidity.

RETURN TO TUSCARORA

Before I tell the next story, I have to preface it with one important piece of background information: I was born in a small town in southern New Jersey, situated along the Delaware River. Okay, keep that in mind, and here we go.

I was invited to return to Tuscarora as the featured speaker for two back-to-back women's retreats. For months I eagerly anticipated the trip. I prayed and asked God to meet me there, once more, just as powerfully and personally as he did the first time. I arrived late at night and was shown to my room overlooking the Delaware River. In the morning, I joyously walked down to the river's edge, hoping to hear from God. But when I looked at the river, my spirit was suddenly in turmoil. I could tell by the leaves on the surface that the water was churning in circles and seemed to be going nowhere. I looked more closely and it appeared to be flowing south to north. *This is madness*, I thought. *I was born on this river. I KNOW it flows north to south!*

I can't describe what happened to me next, other than to say it felt like a panic attack. I literally ran back to my cabin and hid under the covers all day. (The conference didn't start until that evening.) Throughout my first few days at the conference, whenever I wasn't speaking or eating, I was often hiding under the covers. I couldn't understand what was happening to me. I couldn't believe how lethargic I felt. I kept saying to myself, *Snap out of it, girl. This is a momentous occasion. You should be communing with God. You should be on the spiritual high of your life. What's wrong with you?*

One day I went and sat on a bench and prayed, "God, speak to me! I need to hear from you!" and a still, small voice within me said, "You first." I began pouring out my heart to God. I knelt down in the dirt and wept before him, laying down every disappointment, every stupid choice, every broken piece of my shattered life. I laid down everything I had tried to do but had failed at. I laid down my failed marriage. I laid down my hurting children. I laid down my fledgling ministry. I laid it all down and surveyed the ruins, weeping uncontrollably.

Then God brought to my remembrance a scene from my favorite movie, *Out of Africa*. It recounts the true story of Karen Blixen, an author who moved from Denmark to Kenya, hoping to build a better life. Instead, she experienced one catastrophe after another—none of which she signed up for. Her husband made a series of foolish financial decisions, and then abandoned her. Her farm was nearly wiped out by a flood. She recovered, only to have it destroyed by fire.

She began her journey to Africa with high hopes and fine china. She served as benefactress to the local village, providing them with employment and health care. The children had become accustomed to finding little treats in her pockets. But eventually all was stripped away. In the movie, as she watched her farm burn to the ground, a little child ran up and reached into her pocket, but there was nothing there. Karen Blixen stared off into the distance and mumbled softly, "All gone. All gone."

As I knelt in the dirt that day, I mumbled the same words: "All gone. All gone, Father." Gone is all the good advice I thought I could give people. Gone the urge to tell anyone else how to live. Gone every word I felt qualified to speak. Gone the need to build a name for myself. All gone. All gone. I prayed, "Lord, everything I thought I had to offer this world is gone. From now on the only thing I'll give is whatever you give me."

Two days before the conference ended, I walked down to the river again. But this time it was completely different. The current was strong and the river was clearly flowing north to south. "Yes! I knew it!" I wanted to shout! I was so filled with joy, I ran three miles on the scenic road that curves alongside the river, and it felt like a walk around the block.[1] I was completely energized as I took in the beauty of my surroundings: the fall colors everywhere, the sound of leaves crushing under my feet.

Suddenly Hebrews 12:1–2 came to mind, but the Lord personalized it for me: "Therefore since you are surrounded by such a great cloud of witnesses, you need to throw off everything that hinders and the sin that so easily entangles, so you can run with perseverance the race I've marked out for you. Fix your eyes on Jesus, the author and perfecter of your faith."

Later that day God opened my eyes to see the meaning behind my two trips to the river. The first trip symbolized my

---

[1] I should probably mention that I was training for a 5K at the time, so I was certainly capable of running three miles. I had just been too lethargic to do it.

first visit to Tuscarora in 1980. Even though I knew which direction God had told me to go, I chose to go the opposite way, and it threw my life into turmoil. My life was going nowhere. The lethargy symbolized the coping mechanism I used to survive the pain of my marriage. I vividly remember waking up many mornings and just saying, "No. This can't be happening. This can't be my life." Then I'd roll over and try to sleep some more. I was chronically depressed, which lowered my body's immune system and made me chronically sick and barely able to function.

Another thing the Lord showed me was that it would not have upset me to observe the river flowing south to north if I didn't know any better. But since I had been born on that river, I knew in my heart something was wrong. Many people can walk in disobedience to God and not experience inner turmoil. They spend their whole lives blissfully flowing toward hell. But since I had been "born again" along that river, I knew better.

The second trip to the river symbolized my second visit to Tuscarora. This time I not only knew which direction to go, I had the courage and supernatural energy to run with it. And to run with great joy and perseverance. This was God's way of reassuring me that I was now back on track, flowing in the direction he had intended from the beginning.

I had wanted God to speak to me under the moonlight, just as he had during my first trip. So I had stood alone outside on several evenings. Not a peep from God. But on the last night of the conference, as I delivered my talk, God laid it on my heart to invite the ladies to join me down by the river, under the moonlight. I extended the invitation to any who might wish to come to meet me at eleven o'clock. As the moment approached, I wondered if anyone would show up. The enemy was trying to fill my head with the same old lie: "Nobody wants to play with you. These women don't really like you." Approximately seventy-five women gathered together, praying and singing with me along the Delaware River, under the moonlight, until shortly after midnight. It was one of the most beautiful evenings of my life.[2]

As I walked slowly back to my cabin, the Lord gave me the final piece of the puzzle. "The reason you were unable to fulfill my call upon your life the first time is because you stood before me all alone. Now you are surrounded by a great crowd of witnesses—women all around the world who believe in you, pray for you, and want to cheer you on. This time you will run with perseverance the race I've set before you."

TO OBEY IS BETTER THAN SACRIFICE

Another thing God showed me at the river was this: You can't force a river to flow south to north when it was created to flow north to south. The result will be turmoil.

No matter how hard I tried, I could not turn disobedience into obedience. My relationship with my former husband was an act of disobedience from the beginning, but I sincerely thought that if I sacrificed long enough and claimed to be suffering for Jesus (as opposed to suffering for my own stupidity) I could somehow make it look like obedience. It didn't work.

No matter how hard I tried, I could not turn disobedience into obedience.

Am I saying that everyone who deliberately married outside the will of God should rush out and get a divorce as an act of obedience to God? Certainly not! God can and does perform

---

[2] Special thanks to Becky Braisted, Debbie Fawcett, and the wonderful Lutheran Brethren ladies who were part of this life-changing event. I will never forget you, my dear sisters!

marriage miracles on a daily basis. Stories abound of marriages on the brink of ruin yet rescued in response to the faith-filled prayers of one or both partners. There are many couples who had nothing in common, and no human chance to succeed, yet they are thriving, thanks to the grace and mercy of God.

I am not referring to such couples. I am referring to the basket cases, and I am saying let's not spiritualize our predicament. Let's stop pretending we are "suffering for Jesus," when we are simply suffering for our own foolish choices. Let's not claim that God has "allowed this" as a means to "build our character" or that he has placed us there "as a witness." That's exactly the type of thing I used to claim, but I was deceiving myself. God never promotes disobedience, and he never places his children in spiritually compromising positions. We do that on our own. This principle can be applied to every area of our lives, from friendships to finances.

Saul tried to play this little game with God and it didn't work for him either. God had given him very specific instructions.

> "Now go, attack the Amalekites and totally destroy everything that belongs to them. Do not spare them; put to death men and women, children and infants, cattle and sheep, camels and donkeys" (1 Samuel 15:3).

Rather than being completely obedient, Saul spared "the best of the sheep and cattle, the fat calves and lambs—everything that was good" (v. 9).

God sent the prophet Samuel to confront Saul, but rather than being straightforward, Saul tried to play games and make excuses. Watch this:

> When Samuel reached him, Saul said, "The Lord bless you! I have carried out the Lord's instructions."

But Samuel said, "What then is this bleating of sheep in my ears? What is this lowing of cattle that I hear?"

Saul answered, "The soldiers brought them from the Amalekites; they spared the best of the sheep and cattle to sacrifice to the Lord your God, but we totally destroyed the rest" (1 Samuel 15:13–15).

Wow, what a passage! God tells Saul exactly what to do, but Saul has a better idea. Sound familiar? God says, "Kill them all," but that seems so cruel and wasteful. Wouldn't it be better to spare some of those animals? I mean, wouldn't that be better stewardship? Isn't God lucky to have us around, since we know so much more than he does?

I especially love verse 13, where Saul eagerly declares, "I did it for God." Yikes! Sounds like the old Donna! Maybe I'm getting a little cynical in my old age, but I'm at the place now where the more loudly someone insists they're "doing it for God," the higher I raise my eyebrows. The next verse is one of my favorite lines in the entire Bible—I mean, it's just absolutely hilarious when you think about it. Saul insists that he has obeyed God, but Samuel counters, "What then is this bleating of sheep in my ears?"

If Saul had obeyed God—and destroyed everything—he would not be surrounded by sheep, that's for sure.

Saul's circumstances contradict his claim!

Do your circumstances contradict your claims?

Now I'm really making you nervous, huh? Relax! I'm not saying your circumstances are the only measure of your obedience. I'm just asking you a simple question: Is your life filled with the bleating of sheep? That is, the negative logical consequences of your choices (or the choices of those closest to you). Saul chose to let the sheep live; that's why they were bleating. Maybe you chose to let your kids run wild, never taking time out of your hectic schedule to discipline them properly. Now they are living in rebellion. Or maybe you never let them think an independent thought, and *that's* why they're rebelling. Then again, maybe they're just making foolish choices because people routinely make foolish choices and your kids are no exception.

SPIRITUALIZING OUR DISOBEDIENCE

Saul tried to spiritualize his disobedience. Now that he was surrounded by bleating sheep (the circumstances created by his disobedience), he would offer them as a sacrifice to God. He honestly thought that somehow that would make it okay in God's eyes. He figured God would be so pleased with his *sacrifice*, he would overlook the *disobedience*. But that is not what God's Word says! Samuel tells Saul, in verse 22, "To obey is better than sacrifice." More than anything we can give God, be for God, do for God, he simply wants our heart. I very often find that when I have to work too hard at something, it's not from God. Whether it's a friendship I'm trying to work at or a ministry opportunity I'm trying to work at, God's call is to simple obedience. As we obey him, he sends the right people and opportunities our way without undue effort on our part. It shouldn't have to be forced.

More than anything we can give God, be for God, do for God, he simply wants our heart.

OVERTURNED TRASH CAN

If you're like me and you find yourself surrounded by a rather large herd of bleating sheep, you might be feeling discouraged right about now. So let me turn the corner and cheer you up with a little story about my new dog, Bea. Bea is a German shepherd guard dog. And when I say German, I mean she still sleeps in the kennel with the German airline flight sticker on the top. She is ostensibly one of the smartest dogs in the whole world—carefully bred, highly trained, able to do everything except load the dinner dishes into the dishwasher.

Well, Bea was not quite as smart as I had hoped or as highly trained. (I love her anyway, of course!) One Saturday morning I woke up early and decided to make Bea a delicious treat of home-cooked chicken and rice. The reason I have to prepare home-cooked meals for the dog is because twenty years ago I judged my sister-in-law for preparing home-cooked meals for *her* German shepherd. And God never lets me get away with *anything!* I walked into the kitchen and discovered that Bea—one of the smartest, most well-trained dogs in the world, so clever she had to be imported directly from Germany—had snuck into the kitchen the night before and ripped apart the trash bag like some ordinary American mutt.

I brought her into the kitchen and firmly said, "Bad dog!" in German (probably with a really bad German accent, but she got the message anyway). I was so furious with her! She tucked her tail under in disgrace and skulked away to her kennel (the one with the German airline sticker, which we leave on as a daily reminder of just how smart this dog is). I locked her in there so she could ponder her crime for a season.[3]

Well, now I was in a quandary. I fully intended to make Bea a special treat. She had been eating ordinary dog food for several days, and that's expecting a lot, considering what an extraordinary dog she is. So out came the rice cooker and the casserole dish at seven in the morning on a weekend. (If you

---

[3] The dog trainer has since told me my disciplinary technique was incorrect, so if you're a dog lover, rest easy about it.

know anything about me, you know this is a remarkable turn of events.)

It took about forty-five minutes. When everything was ready, I opened the kennel door and encouraged Bea to "come and get it," with my best German accent. She wouldn't come. "You're gonna love it," I promised sweetly. She still wouldn't come. Now I was getting frustrated, because the food I had worked so hard to prepare was just sitting there.

I literally had to drag her out of the kennel and over to the food, which she normally devours. She hung her head and refused to eat. I sat down beside her and began hand-feeding her little pieces of warm chicken, all the while reassuring her that I still considered her a good dog. Eventually she got the idea and enjoyed the rest of the meal.

You see, I was ready to restore our relationship. The fact that she had made a bad choice in no way changed my love for her. True, I had to discipline her. True, I had to allow her to suffer the logical consequences for a season (being confined to her kennel). But I didn't want her locked in there forever; she wasn't eternally doomed. I still wanted her to enjoy good gifts. Unfortunately, she wanted to prolong her punishment beyond what was required.

I have so much in common with animals, sometimes it scares me.

FORGIVING OURSELVES

Just because you've made foolish choices doesn't mean you're a bad person. Or that God hates you and you are doomed to a life of misery. God loves you and he gives second chances. People can learn from their mistakes and become better as a result.

Unfortunately, some people get stuck in a vicious cycle once they've made that first misstep. "When we feel worthless, we act worthless. Instead of faith ruling our lives, insecurity rules our thoughts and actions. We perceive ourselves a certain way, then we act out those perceptions."[4]

You are not the sum of your choices. You are who God says you are.

It's like Bea. Suddenly she saw herself as a junkyard dog and conducted herself accordingly, cowering in her kennel like an enemy of the people. She momentarily forgot that she's an imported wonder-dog, worthy of home-cooked meals. You are *not* the sum of your choices. You are who God says you are:

> But you are a chosen people, a royal priesthood, a holy nation, a people belonging to God, that you may declare the praises of him who called you out of darkness into his wonderful light. Once you were not a people, but now you are the people of God; once you had not received mercy, but now you have received mercy. (1 Peter 2:9–10)

Okay, so you've made some foolish choices. Staying in the kennel with your head hung in shame and your tail tucked between your legs will get you nowhere. God forgives you. He still loves you. Come, enjoy the feast.

YOU'VE GONE FAR ENOUGH IN THAT WAY

Following is the first of several excerpts I want to share with you from a delightful devotional called *Come Away, My Beloved*.[5] Next to my Bible and prayer journal, it is currently

---

[4] Debbie Alsdorf, *Steadfast Love* (Cook Communications, 2000), 56.

[5] I have taken the liberty of updating the language. The original text uses *thee* and *thou*, etc.

my most treasured possession. I have written in the margin of my book, "11/12/01—Nailed me." Read on and see if it nails you too:

> You have made an arduous journey. You have climbed many a mountain that you could easily have walked around. You have often misconstrued My will and felt that only in sacrifice and suffering could you please Me, while much of the time I have longed to deliver you out of the very pains you thus inflicted upon yourself. You meant to please Me but in truth you were only marring your own beauty—which is precious to me.
>
> I cannot rejoice in a blighted rose. You have gone far enough in that way. I offer you My path now, if you are strong enough to accept it. Life and liberty and love and joy. Health and peace—simplicity and rest. It has been there for you all along. You can have it even now if you will.[6]

Ah! Life. Liberty. Love. Joy. Health. Peace. Simplicity. Rest. Now, doesn't THAT sound like the life you signed up for?

GROWTH GUIDE

Key Points to Remember

- One of the reasons we face so many tests is because we pass so many judgments.
- God warns us in advance what will happen when we judge others or violate any of the other fundamental laws of the universe (such as, you reap what you sow).
- When we judge another person, we are putting ourselves in the place of God and we set in motion powerful spiritual

---

[6] Frances J. Roberts, *Come Away, My Beloved* (Ojai, CA: King's Farspan, Inc., 1973), excerpts from 151–52. A hardcover gift edition with language updates is available from Barbour (2002).

forces. It's like whistling for the devil, inviting him to tempt us with the same test we judged others for being unable to withstand.

- Some of us need to make the painful admission that our lives are not where God wants them to be; they are where our own foolish choices have taken us.
- This may not be the life you deliberately signed up for, but if you are honest, it may very well be the logical outcome of your life choices (and the choices of those around you).
- No matter how hard you try, you cannot make disobedience look like obedience!
- God never promotes disobedience, and he never places his children in spiritually compromising positions. We do that on our own.
- Your circumstances are not the only measure of your obedience, but sometimes they do reveal your disobedience in the form of "bleating sheep" (the negative logical consequences of your choices and the choices of those closest to you).

Sometimes we believe God will be so pleased with our sacrifices he will overlook our disobedience. But the Scripture says, "To obey is better than sacrifice."

Application Questions

1. Do you ever feel like God is picking on you? Describe.

2. Does the universe seem like a terribly unjust, confusing place? Why?

3. Have you ever noted a similarity between the number of judgments you pass and the number of trials you face? Do you think there is a connection?

4. Are you a judgmental person? Get a second (and third) opinion before you answer!

5. In what ways have you been "getting back what you've been giving the world"?

6. Can you think of a specific judgment that came back at you? Were you blindsided when the test came?

7. List below the major tests you've faced in life. Now think back. Have you ever judged someone for how they handled that same test? Make the connection!

8. Do you know what it feels like not to be picked? Recall a circumstance when you felt that way.

9. If you are honest, is it possible your life is NOT where God wants it to be but where your own foolish choices have taken you? What were those choices?

10. Have you ever felt like the woman in the scene from *Out of Africa*? Have you ever knelt before God and said, "All gone. All gone"? Do you need to do that right now?

11. Could you identify in any way with my story about the two trips to the river? Describe the ways.

12. Is there a situation in your life where you have previously claimed to be suffering for Jesus but now realize you are simply suffering because of your own foolish choices?

13. Are there any "bleating sheep" in your life?

14. Do your circumstances in life contradict your claims?

15. Have you ever tried to substitute sacrifice for obedience?

16. How did you respond to the story of Bea and the over-turned trash can? Are you in some way trying to prolong your punishment rather than enjoy God's mercy?

Digging Deeper

• Read Romans 2:1–4:

What does this passage say about people who pass judgments?

How do we show contempt for God's kindness?

What is the connection between passing judgment and showing contempt toward God?

- Meditate on Psalm 119:1–48:
  What does the psalmist commit himself to?

  What does he ask God to do for him?

  What do you learn from this passage about "our part" and "God's part" when it comes to avoiding foolish choices?

Look up the following verses and note what you observe about sowing and reaping:

Hosea 8:7

Hosea 10:12

James 2:1–4

James 2:12–13

James 3:18

Psalm 126:5–6

Ecclesiastes 11:6

Proverbs 11:18

2 Corinthians 9:6–11

Galatians 6:7–10

Working It Into Your Life

1. Make a conscious effort to listen to yourself this week. Every time you catch yourself saying or thinking phrases like "I would NEVER" or "I can't believe she ..." or "How could you," write it down. Ask the Lord to make you aware of the judgments you routinely pass on others. Meanwhile, recall times you have used those phrases, and complete each sentence below with some typical words you might say:

   Oh, I can't believe _____

   _____

   How could you _____

   _____

   I would NEVER _____

   _____

2. Spend some time in prayer, asking God to show you any "bleating sheep" in your life. (Remember: Bleating sheep represent the logical negative consequences of your choices.) Be ruthlessly honest. List some of your sheep:

_____   _____

_____   _____

_____   _____

_____   _____

3. If you have a large herd of bleating sheep, go buy yourself a stuffed sheep and keep it in your prayer room as a reminder that your choices have consequences!
4. If you are part of a group, bring your stuffed sheep to class with you and be prepared to talk about one of the "bleating sheep" God revealed to you.

Rewrite One of This Week's Key Verses

_____

_____

_____

_____

_____

_____

_____

Your Prayer in Response

_____

_____

_____

_____

_____

_____

_____

_____

_____

_____

Heavenly Father, I am grateful that you have designed a universe that makes sense. In the past, my life has seemed so chaotic and incomprehensible to me. I thank you for sending your Holy Spirit this week to show me the principle of sowing and reaping. I'm grateful for the knowledge that as I begin to sow differently, I will begin to reap differently. Thank you that Jesus came so that I can have an abundant life instead of a life filled with bleating sheep! Amen.

I didn't sign up for
disappointment
with God

CHAPTER FIVE

I Didn't Sign Up for Disappointment With God

Now to him who is able to do immeasurably more than all we ask or imagine, according to his power that is at work within us, to him be glory in the church and in Christ Jesus throughout all generations, for ever and ever! Amen.

Ephesians 3:20–21

Okay, here's a bold confession for you. I have rarely been disappointed with God, because I have tried my best never to *risk* disappointment with God. See if you can follow me on this. Everyone and everything in my life felt like such a disappointment, I feared that if I asked God for something and he didn't come through, I would totally fall apart. So I played the game of low expectations. (Quick question: Does that sound like faith or fear?)

EVERYTHING WE NEED?

One of my favorite passages is 2 Peter 1:3–9. However, I never fully understood what it actually meant until about half an hour ago as I was standing in the shower letting the conditioner soak in. (I really don't make this stuff up.) Here's the passage:

> His divine power has given us everything we need for life and godliness through our knowledge of him who called us by his own glory and goodness. Through these he has given us his very great and precious promises, so that through them you may participate in the divine nature and escape the corruption in the world caused by evil desires.
>
> For this very reason, make every effort to add to your faith goodness; and to goodness, knowledge; and to knowledge, self-control; and to self-control, perseverance; and to perseverance, godliness; and to godliness, brotherly kindness; and to brotherly kindness, love. For if you possess these qualities in increasing measure, they will keep you from being ineffective and unproductive in your knowledge of our Lord Jesus Christ. But if anyone does not have them, he is nearsighted and blind, and has forgotten that he has been cleansed from his past sins.

Well, in the bad old days (back when I thought I was eternally doomed to stay stuck in the life I didn't sign up for), I always camped out in verse 3. Here's what I thought it meant: God has given us everything we need, so don't be a brat and ask for more. We've got a free trip to heaven and that's a lot more than a significant percentage of the six billion people currently inhabiting the planet. We have God's Word. We have the freedom to worship God. We have great Bible teaching available through our churches, on radio, TV, books. Everything we need to grow in godliness is right there for the taking. So go to church, have your quiet time, read through the Bible every year, buy some good Christian books, and quit complaining.

There's a lot of truth in the above paragraph and it's all very fine and good, as far as it goes. It just doesn't go far enough.

OVERLOOKING THE PROMISES

How I managed to overlook verse 4 is a mystery even to me. I guess I had refined the art of editing out those portions of the Bible that didn't fit with my theology or mindset. Here's my big revelation: It is the PROMISES of God that enable us to "participate in the divine nature and escape the corruption in the world." Hello! That's what it says!

Through the promises, we find the pathway to pleasing God.

Silly me! I thought it was my good doctrine and my determination to "go and sin no more." Yet there it is: Through the promises, we find the pathway to pleasing God. How wild is that? Here I thought I was doing God a big favor by not asking him for anything else. You know, God is busy. Besides, I've had my share of blessings—I mean, hey, I don't live in a Third World country, and I eat out once a week—what right do I have to bother him? Yet over and over, God commands us to ask him for what we need—and stuff we just plain old *want*. I'm including a whole series of Scripture passages just in case anyone reading this is as thickheaded as I am. Hard for some of us to believe, but the Bible really does say:

> "Ask and it will be given to you; seek and you will find; knock and the door will be opened to you. For everyone who asks receives; he who seeks finds; and to him who knocks, the door will be opened" (Matthew 7:7–8).

"Again, I tell you that if two of you on earth agree about any-thing you ask for, it will be done for you by my Father in heaven. For where two or three come together in my name, there am I with them" (Matthew 18:19–20).

"Have faith in God," Jesus answered. "I tell you the truth, if anyone says to this mountain, 'Go, throw yourself into the sea,' and does not doubt in his heart but believes that what he says will happen, it will be done for him. Therefore I tell you, whatever you ask for in prayer, believe that you have received it, and it will be yours" (Mark 11:22–24).

"I tell you the truth, my Father will give you whatever you ask in my name. Until now you have not asked for anything in my name. Ask and you will receive, and your joy will be complete" (John 16:23–24).

Dear friends, if our hearts do not condemn us, we have con-fidence before God and receive from him anything we ask, because we obey his commands and do what pleases him. And this is his command: to believe in the name of his Son, Jesus Christ, and to love one another as he commanded us. Those who obey his commands live in him, and he in them. And this is how we know that he lives in us: We know it by the Spirit he gave us. (1 John 3:21–24)

WHAT ARE YOU ASKING FOR?

I used to look down my spiritual nose at Christians who thought they could go around asking God for whatever they wanted. They just didn't have enough character to be miserable like me! Real Christians aren't into asking for things; we're into suffering, right? Okay, maybe not.

It's taken me twenty-two years to figure out that God really is pleased when we grab hold of his promises. He is pleased when we dare to believe him to do great things. God desires to show himself strong on our behalf. He desires to shower us with good gifts. Let me tell you, folks, this is a whole new approach to the Christian life for me!

Is it possible that the reason you are disappointed with God is because you rarely ask him for anything incredibly wonderful—and as a result, he rarely does anything incredibly wonderful in your life? We are back to the basic spiritual principles that guide the universe. God could just shower you with gifts without your asking. I mean, he's God. Technically speaking, he can do whatever he wants. However, he chooses to act in response to our *faith-filled prayers*. E. M. Bounds, widely recognized as an expert on prayer, has said, "God has chosen to limit his actions on the earth to those things done in direct response to believing prayer."[1] I don't know about you, but that's the most important sentence I've heard in my life. Ponder it. Then put it to the test and see if it isn't so.

God desires to show himself strong on our behalf. He desires to shower us with good gifts.

I believe that to a large extent your Christian walk is a reflection of what you are asking God for. All I ever asked God to do was comfort me in the midst of my suffering. And he did. But until I found within myself the courage to believe God could do more, I was limiting what he could do in my life. If you don't believe God will answer your prayers, you have limited him by your unbelief. Hard to get our brains around that one, but the Bible says it's true. Jesus says to us today the same words he spoke to the two blind men who sought healing two thousand years ago: "According to your faith will it be done to you" (Matthew

---

[1] As quoted by Dr. Dave Earley, *Basic Training for Spiritual Warfare*, New Life Audios, New Life Community Church. Gahanna, Ohio.

9:29). That's not because God loves some Christians more than others; it's not because God is picking on you. It's an inviolable law of the spiritual universe.

For those who have been trapped in a vicious cycle of disappointment and heartache, believing prayer has the power to activate a *positive* cycle of blessing: "Now to him who is able to do immeasurably more than all we ask or imagine, according to his power that is at work within us, to him be glory in the church and in Christ Jesus throughout all generations, for ever and ever! Amen" (Ephesians 3:20–21).

FINDING BALANCE

Now, let's be careful not to turn God into "Our Vending Machine which art in heaven." We cannot get him to do our bidding just by mustering up enough faith. Before you get on your knees and start praying for a new Mercedes, let's come into balance: "You do not have, because you do not ask God. When you ask, you do not receive, because you ask with wrong motives, that you may spend what you get on your pleasures" (James 4:2–3).

Sometimes God loves us so much, he says no, even if it means risking our disappointment. But that's part of being a good heavenly Father. For example, I love my children with all my heart. When they ask me for things, I try to say yes whenever possible. But sometimes I have to love them enough to say no.

My children don't always understand my reasons, but they are learning to trust me enough to handle the word *no* without falling apart. If they do start falling apart, I'll look them in the eye and say, "Receive the no." That's my way of saying, "It's not what you wanted to hear, but it's what you are hearing anyway, so get over it!"

I have a feeling God routinely says "Receive the no" to his children too. Some of us trust him enough to handle it; others fall apart. Which kind of child are you?

Just this morning God gave me a clear illustration of this principle. You've got to believe me when I tell you I don't make this stuff up! I think God allowed it to hammer home a truth he wants me to share with you. Okay, here goes: *Just this morning*, my twelve-year-old asked if she could drive the car! She wasn't happy when I said she couldn't, but I was extremely happy with how quickly she dropped the subject. That right there is a major triumph, let me tell you!

God isn't interested in raising a bunch of spoiled brats. No, God wants to bless us *so that*—repeat, SO THAT—we can be a blessing to others, which brings us to the second half of the passage. You see, it's all about loving God and loving other people.

CHEWING GUM OR BREAD?

Previously, when I linked together the two paragraphs in this passage (2 Peter 1:3–9), I did it like so: Because "God has given us everything we need" (namely, his Son and his Word) we need to "make every effort" to develop the character qualities outlined in verses 5 through 9: faith, goodness, knowledge, self-control, perseverance, godliness, brotherly kindness, and love.

Now, this is a little subtle, but it's significant. When I put forth effort toward my spiritual growth, my approach was to study the Scripture, read books, listen to tapes, attend conferences, all with a view toward increasing my knowledge of God, improving my doctrine, and learning how I was supposed to live my life in a way that would please God. And because I was a diligent student,

I learned a great deal about the character of God and the history of his dealings with mankind. I learned lots of doctrine and guidelines and rules for Christian living.

Yet despite all my vast storehouse of information, I was *not* becoming more like Jesus. In fact, quite the opposite was true. I was becoming a rigid, legalistic jerk. (Don't worry about my using the word *jerk* in a Christian book. It is a biblical term. It comes from the Greek *jerkolopolis*.) It was a long road, but I finally came to the place where I recognized that all my good doctrine had managed to accomplish was to transform me into the kind of person Jesus wouldn't want to spend time with. If our doctrine leads us to reject people Jesus would embrace, then our doctrine is wrong. No matter how many Greek and Hebrew proof-texts you can generate, your doctrine is wrong. Or worse—dangerous to your soul.

Dangerous? How? Because you think you're eating, but you're not! The Word of God wasn't designed to be treated like bubble gum—something you chew on and never digest. Gum is great for blowing bubbles and performing tricks to impress other people. But it doesn't provide any nourishment. It never seeps down into your body to become part of the fabric of your being.

The Word of God wasn't designed to be treated like bubble gum— something you chew on and never digest.

Bread is a whole different food group. The old saying is true: You are what you eat. In this day of rampant bulimia and other eating disorders, it may be necessary for us to rephrase that for greater accuracy: You are what your body digests. I add this clarification because I think there are a great many spiritual bulimics in the church (I was chief among them). A bulimic chews the food, even swallows it, but vomits it back up before it has a chance to digest.

Here's how this hazard was described in the outstanding, must-read book *Empowered Evangelicals*:

> One of the occupational hazards of Bible-based churches is bibliolatry [worshiping the Bible rather than God]. The net effect of such bibliolatry is a depersonalization of God. Eventually, we no longer relate to him. God becomes the object of our investigation . . . the vitality of our religion gets sucked out. As God gets dissected, our stance changes from 'I trust in . . .' to 'I believe that. . . .'[2]

I speak for myself here. I had definitely reduced the Christian life to:

- a list of rules I tried to live by
- a set of beliefs I gave mental assent to

Perhaps you've fallen into the same trap. Knowledge about God is not a substitute for a relationship with God. The issue is never "Am I learning more about God?" It is always "Am I becoming more like him?" Unfortunately, I used my list of rules and my set of beliefs as a tool to evaluate *other people*. If they didn't follow the rules or believe the right things, I wrote them off. The more rules I uncovered, the more so-called truths I learned, the smaller became my list of approved people. The frightening part is there are literally hundreds of thousands of people out there who believe this approach to Christianity is pleasing to God.

Knowledge about God is not a substitute for a relationship with God.

---

[2] Rich Nathan and Ken Wilson, *Empowered Evangelicals* (Ann Arbor, MI: Vine Books, 1995), 139.

We need balance:

> If we emphasize the Word without the Spirit,
>   we dry up.
> If we emphasize the Spirit without the Word,
>   we blow up.
> If we hold the Word and the Spirit together,
>   we grow up.[3]

If you've blown up, you need to get rooted in the Word. If you're drying up, I invite you to consider whether or not you've been guilty of emphasizing the Word without the Spirit—that is, a personal relationship with God is essential, and it is only available through the power of the Holy Spirit living within you.

WHAT'S THE BIBLE FOR?

Last year I attended a four-day recovery program for women emerging from abusive relationships. At the closing ceremony, each woman was invited forward to receive her graduation certificate and a scroll with a Bible verse. The leader said she had prayed over the scrolls (each of which had a unique message) so that even though we were to reach in and randomly select one, she was confident the Holy Spirit would give us exactly what we needed to hear.

Quite frankly, I was skeptical . . . until I read mine. It was one of those moments when you realize the God of the universe is actually following you around. Slightly unnerving, but glorious at the same time. I tell you, my friends, that little piece of paper hit me like the proverbial two-by-four over the head. It was exactly, word for word, what I needed to hear. Maybe it's what you need to hear, as well:

---

[3] Nathan and Wilson, *Empowered Evangelicals,* 53.

Ambitious Conqueror:

Jesus said, "You search the Scriptures, for in them you think you have eternal life, but they are that which testify of Me" [John 5:39–40]. So tell Me: Are you searching the Scriptures to learn facts or to learn of Me?

I have called you to friendship, not frenzy. Life, not legalism! Child, seek to know Me, and in knowing Me you will know the truth as well, for truth transcends mere principle in the same way life transcends biological description. The Scriptures will help you to know Me, yes, but only if you meditate upon them with a listening heart.

Love,
Dad

Knowing what the Bible *says* is a great start.

Knowing what the Bible *means*—that is, having good doctrine—is better.

Knowing how the Bible *applies* to your daily life is better still.

But it's not enough; it must change who we are. I notice a progression in our text for this chapter (2 Peter 1:3–9). We begin to walk by faith and learn to do good things. We increase in knowledge and learn to control our inappropriate behavior. We learn to persevere in our faith and become more godly. But ultimately, the true test of our faith is how we treat other people. We must demonstrate brotherly kindness and love, which are the opposite of the selfishness, harshness, and judgmental attitude demonstrated by a depressing number of Christians today. Such people have forgotten that they've been cleansed from past sins. I should know, because I used to be one of them. Not anymore, though, because I'm finding hope and healing.

The true test of our faith is how we treat other people.

WITHOUT FAITH, IT IS IMPOSSIBLE TO PLEASE GOD

I think the root of the problem stems from trying to manufacture godly character apart from genuine faith. The Scripture says, "Add to your faith." Faith is the cornerstone, the building block upon which all these other character qualities can stand. The Bible plainly says, "Without faith it is impossible to please God" (Hebrews 11:6). *Impossible? Wow!* Strong words.

So what is faith?

Hebrews 11:1 says, "Now faith is being sure of what we hope for and certain of what we do not see."

And what is faith hoping for?

A reward. In fact, the Bible says anyone who comes to God MUST believe that God is going to reward her! Read it yourself: "Anyone who comes to him must believe that he exists and that he rewards those who earnestly seek him" (Hebrews 11:6).

Let's go back to the beginning of this chapter, where I acknowledged my insurance policy against disappointment with God. Namely, "Hope for nothing and you'll never be disappointed." That's not faith; it's resignation. That's not hope; it's despair. I was trying to please God by "adding to my resignation and despair." But without faith, it's impossible to please God. I found that out the hard way. Because try as I might, I could never acquire those other character qualities. In fact, the more I tried and inevitably failed, the more resignation and despair dominated my life.

Like any good writer, God doesn't just *tell* us what faith is; he *shows* us. After defining "faith" in Hebrews 11:1, he devotes the remainder of the chapter to demonstrations of faith in action. "This is what the ancients were commended for" (Hebrews 11:2).

Noah didn't sign up to build an ark. But God asked him to do it, even though there had never been rain on the earth.

Noah didn't wait until he saw the floodwaters rising to spring into action: "By faith Noah, when warned about things not yet seen, in holy fear built an ark to save his family" (v. 7). Noah spent years building that ark, during which time he was the laughingstock of the neighborhood. And I'm sure there were many days when he was tempted to feel disappointed with God, but he didn't give up. His faith was rewarded when he and his family survived the flood, while the rest of civilization was wiped out.

Abraham didn't sign up to leave his home and virtually all of his relatives to go live in a tent in the middle of nowhere. But God asked him to go. Imagine yourself in the foyer at your church next Sunday: "Yeah, Susan, we're moving."

"Where to?"

"We have no idea. We're just moving."

Faith does that kind of crazy thing—*hoping for the best* and absolutely certain of what it cannot see. "By faith Abraham, when called to go to a place he would later receive as his inheritance, obeyed and went, even though he did not know where he was going" (v. 8).

Abraham never did get a new house, but if he was disappointed with God, he didn't let it show. God gave him the reward he wanted most: a son. My daughter Leah was only seven years old when she turned to me one day and declared, "Mommy, Abraham must have REALLY loved God."

"Why is that, sweetheart?"

"Because he gave him his son *twice*."

Leah doesn't miss much.

Sometimes when I'm speaking at a church I'll stay with a host family rather than in a hotel. It's quite a refreshing change, especially when I know I am truly welcome in the home and I am rewarded with delicious home-cooked meals. Last February

I stayed with a middle-aged couple, and the husband absolutely doted upon his wife. You could tell from a mile away how much he adored her. Curious, I asked the wife if it had always been so. "No," she said. "Not until after the cancer." This man's wife nearly died of cancer, but God gave him his wife *twice*, so he was doubly grateful. When I shared with him Leah's insight about Abraham, there were tears in his eyes. This woman didn't sign up for cancer, but she kept the faith and God rewarded her with a second chance at life and a "brand-new" husband.

Sarah didn't sign up to be a barren woman, but God redeemed her tears by giving her a miracle baby in her old age (v. 11). But first he taught her a lesson about laughing when God says he is ready to give us the reward we've wanted for so long.

Moses' parents didn't sign up to surrender their child to the very people who oppressed them as slaves, but their act of faith saved not only the child but an entire nation (v. 23). I can't imagine they are disappointed with God, now that they know how the story ends.

Moses signed up to lead a life of luxury in Pharaoh's palace but wound up spending forty years in the wilderness herding sheep with his father-in-law, and another forty years leading a crowd of complainers through the desert. And after all of that, God forbade him to enter the Promised Land. Moses certainly didn't sign up for any of those disappointments, but he pressed on in faith to the end.

I can't imagine that anyone signed up to be jeered at, tortured, imprisoned, stoned, put to death by sword, or persecuted. But they did not allow the disappointments of life to rob them of their hope and confidence. In the face of all evidence to the contrary, they continued to believe God had something better planned for them (vv. 36–40). And though they didn't get their reward in this lifetime, God is surely lavishing gifts upon them even as we speak. Revelation 2:10 urges us, "Do not be afraid of what you are about to suffer. I tell you, the devil will put some of you in prison to test you, and you will suffer persecution for ten days. Be faithful, even to the point of death, and I will give you the crown of life."

How is it possible that we, who have not faced circumstances nearly so dire, are unwilling to believe God has something better planned for us? I recently had a friend confront me, very forcefully, with an area of sin in my life. I admitted I had never taken it very seriously—it went back to my old attitude that God was probably winking at my sin. My unspoken goal, in so many areas of my life, had always been to see how much I could get away with and still sneak into heaven. Now at last someone had the guts to call me on it. She said, "Don't you realize you're cheating yourself? Don't you realize that someday we will be rewarded for our faithfulness? Isn't it real to you that we will reign with God throughout all eternity and our place in that kingdom will be determined by how faithful we are in this life?"

Every time I do the bare minimum or try to get away with something, I am robbing myself.

Actually no. It had never been real to me before. But as she looked intently at me with tears in her eyes, a giant light bulb went on over my head. There really IS a coming kingdom. I really WILL be rewarded if I continue to walk by faith and live a life that is honoring to God. Every time I do the bare minimum or try to get

away with something, I am robbing myself. If we really have faith in God, no matter how disappointing our life has been thus far, we *must* remain "sure of what we hope for and certain of what we do not see." We must believe that God has a reward for us, both in this life and in the coming kingdom.

A WORD ABOUT TRAGEDY

I want to say a word about tragedy, but I don't want to say too much because I feel unqualified to speak. True, I've had my share of heartache—but most of my pain can be traced back to human choices. Either mine or someone else's. Yet I know there are times in this life when no human explanation can be found.

Margie Erbe knows about tragedy. Margie was miraculously healed of a brain tumor and then lived through hell on earth learning to function again as an adult human being. But God saw her through the experience and then led her into a speaking and writing ministry. She was invited to speak at Arrowhead Ranch, the international headquarters of Campus Crusade for Christ— which is a great honor for a speaker. God told her, very clearly, that this event would be a turning point in her life.

Turning point? she thought. *How exciting. I'm going to bring the whole family.* Shortly after she gave her testimony concerning how God had allowed her to triumph over tragedy, her thirteen-year-old son, Danny, went inline-skating around the campus.

He fell, right there on the holy ground of Arrowhead Ranch.

He fell, hit his head . . . and he died.

I remember Margie calling me early one morning. She didn't say hello. She said, "Danny's dead."

I remember attending the funeral. I remember Margie looking me straight in the eye—looking straight through me—on her way out of the church. I remember it like it happened two seconds ago.

I had nothing to say then. Nothing to say now.

Instead, let me introduce someone who *does* have something profound to say. Philip Yancey, in his amazing book *Disappointment*

With God, quotes his friend Douglas, who has severe debilitating headaches from a car accident:

> I have learned to see beyond the physical reality in this world to the spiritual reality. We tend to think, "Life should be fair because God is fair." But God is not life. And if I confuse God with the physical reality of life—by expecting constant good health, for example—then I set myself up for a crashing disappointment. God's existence, even his love for me, does not depend on my good health. Frankly, I've had more time and opportunity to work on my relationship with God during my impairment than before.[4]

I once worked with a woman who was pregnant with twins. It had been a few years since I'd last seen her, when I bumped into her on the street and enthusiastically inquired about the children. "They both died," she said quietly. "One of the babies lived for eight hours. I treasure the memory of holding her. It was the most precious experience of my life." Thankfully, I was rendered speechless.

My sister works at St. Christopher's Hospital for Children in Philadelphia. The mere thought that there are entire buildings dedicated to sick and dying children is almost more than I can bear. Her area of expertise is hematology-oncology. That is, she works with children with cancer and blood disorders like leukemia and AIDS. Now, with AIDS, we might occasionally be able to point the finger at a drug-addicted parent and "comfort" ourselves that the universe still makes sense. However, most of the suffering she witnesses on a daily basis is inexplicable.

I never have theological discussions with my sister. She says the parents clutching Bibles don't fare any better than the parents

---

[4] Philip Yancey, *Disappointment With God* (Grand Rapids, MI: Zondervan Publishing House, 1988), 183.

who are merely clutching each other. I guess clutching a Bible and being in its clutches are two different things.

But here's the main point I want to make. My sister says—and she of all people should know—"tragedy merely brings out what's already there." It doesn't make the parents stronger. If they are strong, they survive. If they aren't strong, they fall apart. "Some people blame God," she says. "Some people doubt God. The smart ones thank God for allowing them to experience whatever time they DID have with their child."

HOW CHARACTER IS TRANSFORMED

I used to think hardship was the best way to build character. I was wrong. It's certainly one way, but it's not the most effective way. (Yet another brain torque for those of us who specialize in learning everything through painful experience.) The best way to build our character is in meditation upon the promises of God, convincing our hearts of his goodness. That way, if tragedy strikes we will endure. And this much I know for sure: Two months of such meditation has done more to transform my personality than twenty years of look-it-up-and-find-the-right-answer Bible study.

We are not transformed by rising to the occasion. We rise to the occasion because we have been transformed.

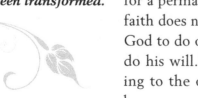

Yancey concludes, "If we insist on visible proofs from God, we may well prepare the way for a permanent state of disappointment. True faith does not so much attempt to manipulate God to do our will as it does to position us to do his will."[5] We are not transformed by rising to the occasion. We rise to the occasion because we have been transformed. How are

5 Ibid., 241.

130

we transformed? By the renewing of our mind. By convincing our heart that God is good, even when our circumstances are not.

GROWTH GUIDE

Key Points to Remember

- Many people are afraid to risk disappointment with God, so they play the game of low expectations (expecting very little from God).
- God chooses to act in response to our faith-filled prayers. To a large extent, your Christian walk is a reflection of what you are asking God for.
- If you don't believe God will answer your prayers, you have limited him by your unbelief.
- God wants to bless us *so that* we can be a blessing to others.
- God's Word is the bread of life, not the chewing gum of life!
- We will reign with God throughout all eternity; our place in the coming kingdom will be determined by our faithfulness here on earth.
- Every time we do the bare minimum or try to get away with something we are robbing ourselves.
- No matter how disappointing our life has been thus far, we must remain sure of what we hope for and certain of what we do not see.
- The best way to build our character is in meditation upon the promises of God, convincing our hearts of his goodness.

Application Questions

1. Do you play the game of low expectations with God to protect yourself from being disappointed?

2. Is it possible that the reason you are disappointed with God is because you rarely ask him to do anything incredibly wonderful for you?

3. In what area of your life have you possibly limited God by your unbelief?

4. Have you ever asked for something with the wrong motives behind it? What was the result?

5. Can you handle it when God says no, or are you inclined to fall apart?

6. Has God ever given you something twice? What impact did that have on your life?

7. What has been your approach to spiritual growth: the chewing gum analogy or bread?

8. Have you ever fallen into bibliolatry: worshiping the Bible rather than God? Have you reduced God to the object of your investigation, so that your Christian life becomes a list of rules you live by and a set of beliefs you give mental assent to?

9. Do you tend to emphasize the Word or the Spirit? Have you ever gotten out of balance? What was the result?

10. Have you observed the dangers of imbalance in other believers? What were the results?

11. Reread the message I received on the scroll. What is your reaction?

12. Is the coming kingdom a compelling reality in your life? Or do you try to see how much you can get away with and still sneak into heaven?

13. Have you experienced tragedy in your life?

14. If so, how did you respond to it initially?

15. Did your response change over time? Explain.

16. Do you believe tragedy makes people stronger or merely brings out what was already there?

Digging Deeper

• Read Genesis 12:1–3:
  What did God ask Abraham to do?

Does God promise to do something for Abraham in return for his act of faith?

What does this passage tell you about the rewards for risks of faith?

- Read Habakkuk 3:17–19:

  Describe the circumstances these people were facing.

  Do these verses tell us something about trusting God when life disappoints us?

  What does God promise to do for those who keep the faith?

- Read 2 Samuel 22:20–37:

  Did you learn something new about the character of God?

  Does God promise anything for those who live uprightly?

- Meditate on Psalm 16:

  What can you have apart from the Lord?

Tell about what God has done/promises to do for us.

What should our response be?

Look up the following verses and note what you learn about faith:

Matthew 6:28–34

Matthew 8:5–12

Matthew 9:27–31

Matthew 13:58

Matthew 17:17–21

Matthew 21:19–22

Mark 6:4–5

Mark 11:22–25

John 14:11–14

Acts 3:16

Working It Into Your Life

1. Choose a passage of Scripture you would like to meditate on. Proverbs 4, especially verses 20–22, is a good start, but feel free to select any passage that ministers to you where you are right now. Write out the passage on an index card or sheet of paper. However, rephrase and personalize it. For example, change "My son, pay attention to what I say" to "Father, I desire to pay attention to your words." Develop the habit of personalizing Scripture; it will greatly enhance your devotional life. Find a quiet place to sit, and begin to read and reread the passage, word by word. Think about every word, every sentence. Be still and open your heart to whatever God wants to show you through this passage. Allow at least thirty minutes for this exercise. If you wish, have your prayer journal on hand to write out anything that comes to mind. However, this is primarily an exercise in meditation.
2. Research some of the people mentioned in the Great Hall of Faith, Hebrews 11. Choose one who is particularly inspiring to you in your life journey right now. If you are part of a small group, be prepared to discuss who you chose and why.

Rewrite One of This Week's Key Verses

_____

_____

_____

_____

_____

Your Prayer in Response

_____

Heavenly Father, thank you for the gift of faith. I ask that through the leading of the Holy Spirit and my diligent determination to heed his voice, I will begin to grow in my faith. I am so thankful for the teachings of Jesus, who demonstrated so clearly what faith looks like and what it can accomplish. Help me to believe that faith can have the same power in my life as it had in New Testament times. My heart's desire is to walk by faith. Amen.

I signed up for happiness

CHAPTER SIX

I Signed Up for Happiness

Do everything without complaining or arguing, so that you may become blameless and pure, children of God without fault in a crooked and depraved generation, in which you shine like stars in the universe as you hold out the word of life—in order that I may boast on the day of Christ that I did not run or labor for nothing.

Philippians 2:14–16

My daughter Leah disappeared for several hours one day last summer. Since she's a homeschooled nature lover, I wasn't completely surprised that she had ventured off outdoors. When she finally came back into the house, I could tell she was excited about some new discovery. "Where've you been?" I asked.

"Watching an anthill," she declared. "Ants are so amazing, Mom! They never stop. You should have seen one of them carrying a great big sunflower seed. *The queen's own children work themselves to death for her!*"

This child's insight never ceases to amaze me. As she stood there breathless in the kitchen, it occurred to me that a lot of *the King's own children* are working themselves to death for him. And when we stop, we feel guilty. Funny thing, though, unlike the queen ant, God doesn't want his children on the run.

If you're anything like me, my guess is you're on the run more often than not. Lots of people, especially good, upstanding Christian people, feel compelled to run around like busy little creatures. It makes us feel important. But it doesn't make us very happy, does it?

I'm quite certain that God would much rather have us sitting at his feet than running self-assigned errands for him. I've made it my goal never to mention Martha or Mary (Luke 10:38–42) in my books, but if I were to mention them, it would be right here. And I think you can pretty much guess what I would say.

Again, in contrast to the queen ant, God doesn't want us carrying giant loads. Instead, he says:

> "Come to me, all you who are weary and burdened, and I will give you rest. Take my yoke upon you and learn from me, for I am gentle and humble in heart, and you will find rest for your souls. For my yoke is easy and my burden is light" (Matthew 11:28–30).

HIS FEET OR SOMEONE ELSE'S DOOR

The problem with carrying around heavy loads is that eventually you've got to set them down somewhere. Or in my case, I used to set them down everywhere. No one could get within a mile of me without hearing a litany of my complaints. The kids weren't listening. I couldn't keep up with my credit card bills. Life on the road was exhausting me; or alternatively, my ministry was in the tank and I wasn't spending enough time on the road. No one loved me anymore. I hated my house. (You know, the one I begged God to give me.) I couldn't keep it and I couldn't sell it. My dog ran away. My car broke down. On and on it went. Negative. Negative. Negative.

Yet I couldn't figure out why my phone never rang. All I wanted to do was spread the misery around. I was doing people a favor, helping them stay in touch with "the real world."

I had one person in particular I liked to complain to because she not only listened sympathetically, she would add little commentary that confirmed she knew the magnitude of my suffering. I'll call her Cindy. I figured it was good for Cindy to listen to my woes since she always had a great big smile on her face and obviously had life "made in the shade." I mean, she never indicated having any problems of her own.

Then one day a mutual friend mentioned in passing that Cindy was dying. "Dying?" I looked at her in astonishment. "As in *dying* dying? But she's only in her forties. How is that possible?" It turns out that Cindy had contracted an incurable disease some five years ago and has been battling it ever since. Cindy is dying. But Cindy is remarkably happy. Unlike me, even though I am not dying and have nothing like her excuse to be unhappy.

Cindy never once mentioned her terminal illness to me in between my sorrowful tales of burnt toast and credit card bills. Although she did share this sage advice with me one day: "You know, Donna, everybody has their own bag of rocks to carry."

And I started to think about that. Everyone has their own bag of rocks. Everyone has their own war stories. Their own heartaches. What right do I have to ask other people to carry *my* bag in addition to their own? What right did I have to burden this dying woman with my never-ending negativity?

No right at all. That's why Jesus told us to lay our burdens down at his feet, to make it easier for us to resist the temptation to lay them down at everyone else's door.

HOW HAPPY DO YOU WANT TO BE?

You know how sometimes you hear a pithy little expression and you wish you hadn't? I once heard it said, "Most people are pretty much as happy as they've made up their minds to be." Ouch. I didn't like that at all. 'Cause, frankly, I was miserable. And it's bad enough to be miserable without being blamed for your own misery.

Wouldn't you know, it turns out to be true? The world is a great big place, and our experience of the world hinges on one very simple decision we make every day: What will we focus on?

We can choose to focus on what's right with the world and be happy.

We can choose to focus on what's wrong with the world and be miserable. Or we can choose to focus on what's right with the world and be happy.

Cindy hops out of bed in the morning and says, "I'm alive today. That's a good thing. I'm happy about that." I drag myself out of bed and say, "I have fat thighs. That's a bad thing. I'm unhappy about that."

Two women. Two choices. One happy. The other unhappy.

Life is a funny thing.

MAGNIFYING GLASS

Imagine that you are standing next to a gigantic poster filled with a wide variety of tiny little images—some beautiful, some frightening; some bright, some dark. Now imagine that you have a magnifying glass in your hand. What will determine the type of images you see? Where you point your magnifying glass.

Every moment of every day has good and bad in it. Every person you meet has strengths and weaknesses. Every situation has pros and cons. Every event contains both the handiwork of God and the counterattack of the enemy. Even the life you didn't sign up for is filled with things you *did* sign up for, when you stop and think about it.

The question is: What will you choose to magnify? It's entirely up to you. Keep in mind: Whatever you focus your magnifying glass on will appear larger than everything else. When you choose to magnify the bad, it appears larger than it really is. But when you choose to magnify God, you get a clearer picture of reality. You realize that God is larger than your problems. Here's how the psalmist put it:

> I will bless the Lord at all times;
> His praise shall continually be in my mouth.
> My soul shall make its boast in the Lord;
> The humble shall hear of it and be glad.
> Oh, *magnify* the Lord with me,
> And let us exalt His name together. (Psalm 34 NKJV)

Webster's Dictionary defines *magnify*: "to make great in representation; to extol; to exalt in description or praise. To elevate; to raise in estimation; to increase the apparent dimensions." The New International Version of the Bible renders the word *magnify* "exalt," which *Webster's* defines: "to elevate with joy or confidence."

When you choose to magnify God rather than your problems, you elevate God with joy and confidence. Isn't that perfect? Not in resignation. Not as a Pollyanna, who denies the reality of the situation. Instead, with confidence in God's goodness, you can approach life in a healthy, balanced way that acknowledges the heartaches and disappointments of life but still chooses to see God's redemptive power at work.

COMPLAINING

The opposite of magnifying God is complaining. It has been observed that complaining is like whistling for the devil. So unless you want the enemy to show up on your doorstep, you'd better stop complaining. The first time I took the sin of complaining seriously was when I read the following passage and realized how seriously God takes it:

Now the people complained about their hardships in the hearing of the Lord, and when he heard them his anger was aroused. Then fire from the Lord burned among them and consumed some of the outskirts of the camp. When the people cried out to Moses, he prayed to the Lord and the fire died down. So that place was called Taberah, because fire from the Lord had burned among them.

The rabble with them began to crave other food, and again the Israelites started wailing and said, "If only we had meat to eat! We remember the fish we ate in Egypt at no cost—also the cucumbers, melons, leeks, onions and garlic. But now we have lost our appetite; we never see anything but this manna!"

The manna was like coriander seed and looked like resin. The people went around gathering it, and then ground it in a handmill or crushed it in a mortar. They cooked it in a pot or made it into cakes. And it tasted like something made with olive oil. When the dew settled on the camp at night, the manna also came down.

Moses heard the people of every family wailing, each at

the entrance to his tent. The Lord became exceedingly angry, and Moses was troubled. He asked the Lord, "Why have you brought this trouble on your servant? What have I done to displease you that you put the burden of all these people on me? Did I conceive all these people? Did I give them birth? Why do you tell me to carry them in my arms, as a nurse carries an infant, to the land you promised on oath to their forefathers? Where can I get meat for all these people? They keep wailing to me, 'Give us meat to eat!' I cannot carry all these people by myself; the burden is too heavy for me. If this is how you are going to treat me, put me to death right now—if I have found favor in your eyes—and do not let me face my own ruin" (Numbers 11:1–15).

Notice how complaining affects the people around us who are trying to keep a positive attitude. Other people's complaining made Moses so miserable he wanted to die. He had too many people asking him to carry their bag of rocks.

God takes our complaints seriously, and he takes them personally. In Philippians 2:14–16, he commands us:

Do everything without complaining or arguing, so that you may become blameless and pure, children of God without fault in a crooked and depraved generation, in which you shine like stars in the universe as you hold out the word of life—in order that I may boast on the day of Christ that I did not run or labor for nothing.

THE POWER OF AFFIRMATIONS

Recently a friend encouraged me to compile a list of daily affirmations—positive words I speak aloud that reflect not where I am right now but where I want to go and who I want to be. It's been a wonderful addition to my prayer time each day. I feel confident that I am becoming a happier person as a result of this simple exercise. Let me share some of my affirmations with you. They are very personal—I'm really giving you a glimpse into the deepest desires of my heart here. If you are ever wondering how you might pray effectively for me, you can pray that I would truly become the woman described below, even as you pray that these things would be true in your own life:

- I know today will be a great day, because God's mercies are new every morning. (Lamentations 3:23)
- No weapon that is formed against me today will prosper. All those who rise up against me will fall. Every accusation made against me will be refuted. (Isaiah 54:17)
- The enemy may come against me one way, but he'll be forced to flee from me seven ways! (Deuteronomy 28:7)
- Today I will know firsthand the love of Christ, which passes knowledge, and I will be filled with the fullness of God. (Ephesians 3:19)
- I'm not going to be afraid of anything today. Because God has not given me a spirit of fear but of love, power, and a sound mind. (2 Timothy 1:7)
- I can either magnify God or magnify my problems. I choose to magnify God. (Psalm 69:30–31)
- This family is blessed when we come in and blessed when we go out. (Deuteronomy 28:6)
- I have absolutely no regrets about my life. Everything that's happened to me, even the pain, will be redeemed and turned into something good. (Romans 8:28)

- I never complain, because I refuse to whistle for the devil. (Philippians 2:14)
- I never complain, because it robs me—and everyone around me—of joy. Besides, the world doesn't need any more verbal pollution. (Philippians 2:14)
- I always remember: She who guards her mouth and her tongue keeps herself from trouble. (Proverbs 21:23)
- I always choose to offer the sacrifice of praise and thanksgiving (Hebrews 13:15). God inhabits praise. The enemy inhabits negativity. I choose God. And I choose to praise him.
- I never make excuses for my behavior. All that does is keep me stuck in my old ways. (1 John 1:8–9)
- I know that life and death are in the power of the tongue. So may the words of my mouth and the meditation of my heart be acceptable before God. (Psalm 19:14)
- I never judge anyone, because I know everyone is doing the best they can. And I don't know everyone's story. (Matthew 7:1)
- I never curse or condemn anyone, because I want to keep God's blessings flowing into my life. (Luke 6:37)
- If people could sum me up in one word, I hope it would be *gracious*. I always seek to extend to others the same grace God has extended to me. (Ephesians 4:29–32)
- I am becoming more and more like Jesus all the time: gracious, generous, anointed, and compassionate. I walk moment by moment in the power of the Holy Spirit. (2 Corinthians 3:17–18)

RE-CREATING ATMOSPHERE

I believe the reason my daily recitation of affirmations is hav-ing such a powerful impact on my life is because it is resetting my emotional thermostat. Let me explain. You set a thermostat to 70 degrees or whatever temperature feels most comfortable for you. Then when the temperature in the room reaches above or drops below that point, the air-conditioning/heating unit automatically kicks in to bring the room back to the selected temperature.

Our emotional thermostats are set at a very young age. If you grew up in a quiet, peaceful, loving home, your tempera-ture is probably set around 72 degrees. Not too hot. Not too cold. That's one of the reasons why people raised in Christian homes—and especially those whose families have been believers for generations—have very peaceful lives.

However, if you were raised in a non-believing home, espe-cially if it was a home filled with chaos and conflict, your emo-tional thermostat is set around 85 degrees. Maybe even higher. And this is the key: When life cools down a bit, something inside of you will *automatically* kick in to raise the temperature. You will unconsciously look for ways to heat things up! To stir up trouble. To get that adrenaline rushing. You re-create the atmosphere that feels most familiar.

I did this constantly. If I didn't have a crisis, I'd invent one. If I wasn't embroiled in conflict with someone, I'd pick a fight. I was always poised for battle. As a result, I invariably managed to find a worthy opponent. If I didn't have something at the moment to make me unhappy, I would look for something to be unhappy about.

I was continually in a state of turmoil, continually working myself into a frenzy. But God has clearly called me—just as he has called you—to reset the thermostat to a peaceful temperature.

He has called us to quietness and rest. He has called us to happiness.

> I don't want you to work for Me under pressure and tension like a machine—striving to produce, produce. I want you to just LIVE with ME as a PERSON. I have waited for you to wear yourself out. I knew you would find it eventually—the secret of silence and rest, of solitude and of song. I will rebuild your strength—not to work again in foolish frenzy, but just for the sake of making you strong and well. To Me this is an end in itself. Make it your aim and join with Me wholeheartedly in this project. Many joys are waiting yet.[1]

Do you believe many joys are waiting for you? Indeed, you are surrounded by a multitude of people and places that could fill your heart with happiness every day. All you have to do is open your eyes and see the good. Right now, you can choose to enjoy the happiness you signed up for. What are you waiting for?

GROWTH GUIDE

Key Points to Remember

- The problem with carrying heavy loads is that, eventually, you've got to set them down somewhere. Everyone has her own bag of rocks to carry. We have no right to ask someone else to carry ours as well.
- Jesus told us to lay our burdens down at his feet, to make it easier for us to resist the temptation to lay them down at everyone else's door.

---

[1] Roberts, *Come Away, My Beloved*, 152.

- Most people are pretty much as happy as they've made up their minds to be.
- Our experience of the world largely depends on what we choose to focus on: We can focus on what's wrong with the world and be miserable, or we can focus on what's right with the world and be happy.
- When we choose to magnify the bad, it appears larger than it really is. But when we choose to magnify God, we begin to get a clearer picture of reality.
- When we choose to magnify God, we remind ourselves that God is larger than all our problems.
- With confidence in God's goodness, we can approach life in a healthy, balanced way that acknowledges the heartaches and disappointments of life but still chooses to see God's redemptive power at work.
- Complaining is the opposite of magnifying God. It's like whistling for the devil.
- Each of us has an emotional thermostat, which was set at a very young age. We subconsciously work to re-create the temperature that feels most familiar.

Application Questions

1. Do you feel compelled to run around like a busy little creature? Does it make you feel important? Do you feel unimportant if you are not busy?

2. Do you work yourself to death for your King? How does

it affect your relationship with him? How does it affect your happiness?

3. Do you carry around heavy loads . . . and routinely set them down at other people's doors?

4. In what way do you ask other people to carry your bag of rocks in addition to their own?

5. Is there one person in particular you like to complain to? How do you think that affects your relationship?

6. Do you know someone like Cindy—someone with every reason to complain but who keeps a great attitude in the midst of a deep trial? Describe.

7. How has this person's positive attitude affected you and the people around her/him?

8. How would this person's influence be different if he/she constantly complained about the situation?

9. Do you tend to focus on what's right with the world—or what's wrong with it? In other words, where do you direct your magnifying glass?

10. What is the result of focusing your attention as you do?

11. How has your complaining affected people around you who were trying to keep a good attitude?

12. How do you react to the statement "Complaining is like whistling for the devil"? Explain.

13. What temperature is your emotional thermostat set at? Explain.

14. Do you ever heat things up in your life when things get too peaceful?

15. Alternatively, do you panic when things naturally heat up and seek to lower the temperature no matter the cost?

Digging Deeper

- Read Psalm 1:1–6:
  Describe the lifestyle of one who is blessed:

  Contrast the lifestyle of the wicked:

  What are the benefits enjoyed by the one who is blessed by God?

- Meditate on Psalm 34:
  List all the things the psalmist magnifies about God:

Look up the following Scriptures and note what you discover about happiness and/or things we should be happy for. (Some translations render *happy* as *blessed*. If you are so inclined, look up both words in a dictionary.)

Ecclesiastes 2:24–26

Psalm 32:1–2

Psalm 94:12

Proverbs 3:13–18

Proverbs 8:34–36

Proverbs 16:20

Luke 1:45

James 1:12

Revelation 1:3

Working It Into Your Life

1. Locate a magnifying glass and put it in your prayer room as a visual reminder that we can choose, each day, what we will magnify.
2. Find a picture or poster with a lot of detail in it. If you are part of a weekly small group, bring your picture to class and experiment with focusing on different parts of

the picture to illustrate how we can focus on the bright and the positive in life.

3. Keep an eye on your emotional thermostat this week.
4. Read the affirmations found in the back of this book. Cut out the ones that help you, or write some of your own. Keep them where you'll see them frequently and develop a habit of reading them daily.
5. Make a list of ten things you have to be thankful for and recite them daily!

_____   _____

_____   _____

_____   _____

_____   _____

_____   _____

Rewrite One of This Week's Key Verses

_____

_____

_____

_____

_____

_____

_____

Your Prayer in Response

_____

_____

_____

_____

_____

_____

_____

_____

_____

_____

*Heavenly Father, I thank you for the truth that I can
be as happy as I choose to be. You have blessed me
in every conceivable way, most of all by sending your
Son to die on a cross for me. Above all the "things"
I ask for in prayer, all the "things" I think I need to
make me happy, Lord, I ask right now for a thankful
heart. In Jesus' name. Amen.*

I signed up for
great health

CHAPTER SEVEN

I Signed Up for Great Health

Jesus went through all the towns and villages, teaching in their synagogues, preaching the good news of the kingdom and healing every disease and sickness.

Matthew 9:35

Since we have these promises, dear friends, let us purify ourselves from everything that contaminates body and spirit, perfecting holiness out of reverence for God.

2 Corinthians 7:1

In one sense, I am completely unqualified to write this chapter, because I was chronically ill for twenty years. Even though I didn't have a life-threatening illness, I was frequently under the weather, and often was flat-out down for the count. I have had two different occasions where friends showed up at my house and found me delirious with fevers hovering around 104 degrees. One of these women told a mutual friend she'd never seen anyone look so near death in her life.

In another sense, I am eminently qualified to write about it because I know what it feels like to be sick all the time. If you're anything like me, you are sick and tired of feeling sick and tired. Or maybe someone in your life is chronically ill and your life has been profoundly affected by their suffering.

Although this chapter will not be definitive by any stretch of the imagination, I'd like to share with you what God has shown me about the various causes of sickness, along with the prescription I am pursuing in my own life. Maybe together we can discover the path to the great health we signed up for.

THE SUFFERING OF JOB

Quoting from the book of Job is always a tricky business because more than half of the dialogue is included for the express purpose of exposing wrong-headed thinking. I don't know about you, but that makes me fear quoting it in some wrong-headed fashion. But how cowardly can I be? To write an entire book entitled *This Isn't the Life I Signed Up For* and not tackle Job? *Tsk. Tsk.* So while I am quaking in my boots, let's read a selection together:

> On another day the angels came to present themselves before the Lord, and Satan also came with them to present himself before him. And the Lord said to Satan, "Where have you come from?"
>
> Satan answered the Lord, "From roaming through the earth and going back and forth in it."
>
> Then the Lord said to Satan, "Have you considered my servant Job? There is no one on earth like him; he is blameless and upright, a man who fears God and shuns evil. And he still maintains his integrity, though you incited me against him to ruin him without any reason."
>
> "Skin for skin!" Satan replied. "A man will give all he has

for his own life. But stretch out your hand and strike his flesh and bones, and he will surely curse you to your face."

The Lord said to Satan, "Very well, then, he is in your hands; but you must spare his life."

So Satan went out from the presence of the Lord and afflicted Job with painful sores from the soles of his feet to the top of his head. Then Job took a piece of broken pottery and scraped himself with it as he sat among the ashes.

His wife said to him, "Are you still holding on to your integrity? Curse God and die!"

He replied, "You are talking like a foolish woman. Shall we accept good from God, and not trouble?" (Job 2:1–10).

SICKNESS CAN BE DUE TO SATANIC AFFLICTION

Before launching into this, let me say that I'm in the enviable position of not having a theological ax to grind. There will be something in the following paragraphs for everyone to dispute. It's not important for you to agree with me; what matters is that you begin to get God's perspective and move a step closer to experiencing the life you signed up for. All I'm asking is that you prayerfully consider what I'm about to say.

When the Bible tells us something clearly, we don't need to start reading between the lines or trying to explain things away because they make us uncomfortable. In this case, the Bible tells us *exactly* what happened. Job was the most righteous man living on the earth at the time. Satan asked for permission to afflict him and God granted him that permission, even though God himself says Job had done nothing wrong to provoke it. "Satan went out from the presence of the Lord and AFFLICTED Job with painful sores from the soles of his feet to the top of his head" (Job 2:7, emphasis added). Obviously our enemy has the power to afflict people with sickness. He can even afflict nice, upstanding Christians. And God lets him do it. I don't understand it. I don't particularly like it. But that's what it says.

Jesus himself addressed the difficult and perplexing issue of human suffering:

> As He went along, He saw a man blind from birth. His disciples asked Him, "Rabbi, who sinned, this man or his parents, that he was born blind?"
>
> "Neither this man nor his parents sinned," said Jesus, "but this happened so that the work of God might be displayed in his life" (John 9:1–3).

Jesus clearly states that sickness is NOT always the result of sin, as some teachers today claim. Sometimes God allows physical disability for a specific purpose. In this instance, this man's life demonstrated to the Pharisees (and whoever else would listen) that spiritual blindness is worse than physical blindness. Physical blindness is temporary, but spiritual blindness is eternal hell.

The following example of a physical handicap for God's glory is written by Arthur Christopher Bacon and quoted by L. B. Cowman in her devotional book *Streams in the Desert* (February 12):[1]

> A visitor at a school for the deaf was writing questions on the board for the children. Soon he wrote this sentence: "Why has God made me able to hear and speak, and made you deaf?"
>
> The shocking sentence hit the children like a cruel slap on the face. They sat paralyzed, pondering the dreadful word "Why?" And a little girl arose. With her eyes swimming with tears, she walked straight to the board. Picking up the chalk, she wrote with a steady hand these precious words: "Yes,

[1] L. B. Cowman, *Streams in the Desert* (Grand Rapids, MI: Zondervan, updated 1999).

Father, for this was your good pleasure" (Matthew 11:26). What a reply! It reaches up and claims an eternal truth upon which the most mature believer, and even the youngest child of God, may securely rest—the truth that God is your Father.

IS ALL SUFFERING NOBLE?

I grew up believing that suffering of any kind—including sickness—was inherently noble. It was a badge of honor, a form of martyrdom. It was a sign that you were a giant of the faith, like Job, because God knew he could entrust you with suffering and you wouldn't "curse God and die." I once heard a message entitled "Can God Trust You?" and it really had an impact on me. *Yes*, I thought. *I want to be someone God can trust. I don't want to be a fair-weather friend of God, who only accepts good from his hand and not trouble.* I'm glad I heard that message and took it to heart. I think it's made me a better person, less of a spiritual wimp than I otherwise would have been. But I think I took it to the extreme and passively accepted suffering that God never intended me to endure. I tended to lie down and die, when God wanted me to stand and fight.

Although no one came out and confirmed it, I've attended churches where the most admired people were those who suffered the most. This theological line of thought is rooted in the book of Job. God deliberately brings Job to Satan's attention as a stellar example of faithfulness. God says, in essence, "Of all my servants, this is one you can put to the test, because I know he will do me proud." So whenever we saw Christians who were sick or suffering, we assumed that a similar conversation had taken place in heaven, with God saying to Satan, "There's another of my best and brightest. Go put her to the test."

The New Testament also lends support to this perspective:

> Consider it pure joy, my brothers, whenever you face trials of many kinds, because you know that the testing of your faith develops perseverance. Perseverance must finish its work so that you may be mature and complete, not lacking anything. (James 1:2–4)

Even Jesus was not exempt from suffering (although it's interesting to note there is no mention in Scripture of Jesus experiencing sickness):

> During the days of Jesus' life on earth, he offered up prayers and petitions with loud cries and tears to the one who could save him from death, and he was heard because of his reverent submission. Although he was a son, he learned obedience from what he suffered and, once made perfect, he became the source of eternal salvation for all who obey him. (Hebrews 5:7–9)

THE EXCEPTION OR THE RULE?

Clearly God sometimes allows sickness and physical disability. And it's equally clear that such suffering brings out the best in some people. They seize the opportunity to find God in the midst of their pain. But let's be honest and come into balance here: Chronic illness can also warp our character rather than build it. For every Joni Eareckson Tada, there are countless thousands of self-consumed sick people whose only topic of conversation is their current symptoms. I should know, because that's exactly what happened to me. My chronic illness did not turn my eyes toward God; it turned my gaze inward. Proverbs 18:14 points out, "A man's spirit sustains him in sickness, but a crushed spirit who can bear?" In other words, it can really wear you down after a while. Or, as mentioned previously, suffering of any variety often brings to the surface what is already inside of us. That's why the Scripture says, "Above all else, guard your heart, for it is the wellspring of life" (Proverbs 4:23).

Although there are obvious exceptions (as noted above), the lives of God's favored children throughout the Old Testament were typically characterized by health and long life. Throughout Scripture, sickness is frequently portrayed not as a test of faithfulness but as a curse or the consequence of disobedience. When the Israelites entered the Promised Land, God warned them about this very thing:

> If you do not carefully follow all the words of this law, which are written in this book, and do not revere this glorious and awesome name—the Lord your God—the Lord will send fearful plagues on you and your descendants, harsh and prolonged disasters, and severe and lingering illnesses. He will bring upon you all the diseases of Egypt that you dreaded, and they will cling to you. The Lord will also bring on you every kind of sickness and disaster not recorded in this Book of the Law, until you are destroyed. (Deuteronomy 28:58–61)

The above passage clearly says sickness is sometimes sent as a punishment for disobedience. Now don't panic. I didn't say *always*. I said *sometimes*.

I've heard people say that God allowed an illness—or even that he sent an illness—in order to get their attention so that they would make changes in their lives. Although it is certainly true that sickness often forces us to stop and take a hard look at our lives, wouldn't it be better to look before we wound up in a hospital bed? As the authors of *Empowered Evangelicals* put it, "Far better to be made holy through prayer and Bible reading,

"Far better to be made holy through prayer and Bible reading, fellowship, worship, and obedience to the commandments of God."

fellowship, worship, and obedience to the commandments of God than through the brokenness caused by the fall."[2]

The following passages are typical of the lifestyle of Jesus:

> Jesus went through all the towns and villages, teaching in their synagogues, preaching the good news of the kingdom and healing every disease and sickness. (Matthew 9:35)

> When the sun was setting, the people brought to Jesus all who had various kinds of sickness, and laying his hands on each one, he healed them. (Luke 4:40)

I can't help but notice what these verses *don't* say. They don't say Jesus went around making people sick so they could prove how much faith they had or to get their attention. Quite the opposite. He made it one of his primary missions to heal people and repeatedly said, "Your faith has made you well" (Luke 17:19). He never once said, "Your faith has allowed you to get sick."

There is a single instance recorded where Jesus apparently allowed someone to get sick and die, and it was done for the express purpose of glorifying God. But notice, it was not the sickness (and ultimate death) that glorified God; it was the healing and resurrection that glorified God:

> Now a man named Lazarus was sick. . . . So the sisters sent word to Jesus, "Lord, the one you love is sick." When he heard this, Jesus said, "This sickness will not end in death. No, it is

---

2 Nathan and Wilson, *Empowered Evangelicals*, 80.

for God's glory so that God's Son may be glorified through it" (John 11:1, 3–4). [As you know, Lazarus died and Jesus raised him from the dead.]

IS SICKNESS THE RESULT OF A LACK OF FAITH?

So what shall we conclude? Clearly Jesus had a passion for healing the sick. And since he is the same yesterday, today, and forever, we can be certain he still desires to heal the sick among us. I think it's obvious that a loving heavenly Father would generally want his children to be healthy, just as a loving earthly father would. Can you imagine a parent injecting her child with the flu to teach him a lesson or to get his attention? Certainly not! What do we do with parents who deliberately inflict pain on their children? We lock them up as child abusers.

Here again, Christians go to extremes. Some teach that if we have enough faith, we will never be sick throughout our entire lifetime. If we are sick, there is invariably a lack of faith involved. But what can we say about a three-year-old girl who dies of leukemia? That she has somehow committed some wicked deed? Impossible! Or that she's being punished for the sins of her parents? Why are healthy babies found in trash cans? If God were going to punish wickedness with birth defects, these people would be giving birth to seriously deformed kids. Can we say that she or her parents lack faith? Plenty of atheists and agnostics give birth to healthy children, so it's hardly a cause-effect relationship.

I once attended a Bible study with a young woman who'd been left devastated after her baby was born anencephalic (without a brain). But her church said if she had enough faith, her baby would live. She believed with all her heart that God was going to perform a miracle, but her baby died. Sadly, she lost not only her baby but also her standing in the church. She almost lost her grip on sanity, not to mention her faith.

Eighty percent of all church prayer requests are related to sickness.

Lack of faith is not the only explanation for the heartaches of life. It definitely explains some things, but not everything. Repeat: Lack of faith is *not* the only explanation for the heartaches of life.

What I'm trying to advocate here is some kind of balance . . . and may God help me! I know I'm walking into the middle of the fray. I was tempted to delete this entire chapter, because I know I'm stepping all over people's toes. But how could I possibly discuss "the life I didn't sign up for" without addressing sickness? A national Christian magazine surveyed pastors and discovered that 80 percent of all church prayer requests are related to sickness. My own sense, just from thirty years hanging around church, is that this estimate is accurate. So we need to get a grip on this issue.

It would seem to me that the healthiest view of sickness (if you'll pardon the pun) is to view it "chiefly as a consequence of the ... universal human experience of fallenness and not primarily as sent to us by God to make us holy."[3] Not, I might add, as a result of a lack of faith on our part.

We live in a fallen world, not the best of all possible worlds. The garden of Eden is a distant memory. Today the garden is filled with pesticides, not to mention the fallout of nuclear bombs and other toxic waste. In my own case, I grew up playing in a wooded lot near my home that was later declared a Super-Fund Site by the Environmental Protection Agency (meaning it was so toxic, it was a top priority for cleanup). My extended family is riddled with cancer, but I sincerely doubt the cause

---

[3] Ibid., 80.

is a family curse or lack of faith. A more likely explanation is that we lived in a highly industrial area of the northeastern United States.

Shortly after writing the above paragraph, I stumbled upon the following article on the Internet:

> Long-term exposure to the air pollution in some of America's biggest metropolitan areas significantly raises the risk of dying from lung cancer and is about as dangerous as living with a smoker, a study of a half-million people found. The study echoes previous research and provides the strongest evidence yet of the health dangers of the pollution levels found in many big cities and even some smaller ones, according to the researchers from Brigham Young University and New York University.[4]

No doubt about it, folks. We live in a fallen world, and that has major ramifications for our health.

SICKNESS CAN BE A LOGICAL CONSEQUENCE OF OUR LIFESTYLE

In many instances, sickness is nothing more than the logical consequence of our lifestyle. We don't need to look for profound supernatural explanations when plain old common sense will do. I'm not going to devote too much time to this point, because I think it is self-explanatory. Nevertheless, it is extremely significant. Don't let the length of the paragraph fool you into underestimating its importance. Poor diet and lack of exercise account for a wide range of common ailments. Many people neglect their physical body, and then blame God or the devil when they become ill. If you are fifty pounds overweight and think

---

[4] *Associated Press* report on the Internet, March 5, 2002.

lifting the potato chip from the bag to your mouth is a workout, you don't need to ponder whether or not Satan is afflicting you. You are afflicting yourself. And there is nothing noble about that kind of suffering.

I recently received an e-mail from a woman who has totally turned her life around by changing her lifestyle. Joan Paterson attended one of my conferences and e-mailed me afterward telling me her marriage was in trouble. I felt led to ask her how she felt about herself. "Terrible" was the response. She was overweight and chronically sick. Apparently I inspired her to transform her health through diet and exercise. She lost fifty-five pounds, saved her marriage, and says she has never felt better in her life. I am quite certain one of the factors in my chronic sickness is my addiction to carbohydrates, coupled with my aversion to vegetables. God has convicted me that it's not enough to pray for healing; I have to modify my eating habits. My guess is that nine out of ten women reading this could benefit by a change in their diet and exercise habits.[5]

SICKNESS CAN BE ROOTED IN EMOTIONAL PAIN

There are other ways to abuse our physical bodies besides neglecting exercise. Medical science continues to confirm that many illnesses are rooted in emotional pain, which manifests itself in physical pain. There are exceptions, of course, but many diseases can be traced back to anxiety and stress. Long-term, low-level anxiety has been directly linked to cancer. High levels of stress are clearly the primary cause of heart attacks. I recently read an alarming statistic about the number of women in abusive relationships who contract breast cancer. Other

---

[5] Check out my book *Becoming the Woman I Want to Be: A 90-Day Journey to Renewing Spirit, Soul, and Body* (Bethany House, 2004).

studies have linked breast cancer to post-abortion syndrome. That's not to say that all breast cancer victims are in abusive relationships or have endured the heartbreak of abortion, but who can deny that emotional pain eventually takes a toll on the body?

God has created us as triune creatures: spirit, soul, and body. First Thessalonians 5:23 says, "May your whole spirit, soul and body be kept blameless at the coming of our Lord Jesus Christ." And 2 Corinthians 7:1 reminds us, "Since we have these promises, dear friends, let us purify ourselves from everything that contaminates body and spirit, perfecting holiness out of reverence for God."

Many diseases can be traced back to anxiety and stress.

Whatever impacts one part of our being impacts the other two parts as well. If we neglect our spirit, then our soul and body suffer. If we neglect our soul (mind, will, and emotions), then our spirit and body suffer. And if we neglect our body, it typically has a *negative—not positive*—effect on our spirit and soul. Isn't that just common sense?

Consider these words from *Come Away, My Beloved*:

> How can I give you healing for your body while there is anxiety in your mind? So long as there is dis-ease in your thoughts, there shall be disease in your body. You have need of many things, but one thing in particular you must develop for your own preservation and that is an absolute confidence in my loving care.
>
> "Come unto Me," it is written, "all ye that labor and are heavy-laden, and I will give you rest" (Matthew 11:28). Only when your mind is at rest can your body build health. Worry is an actively destructive force. Anxiety produces tension, and tension is the road to pain. Fear is devastating to the physical

well-being of the body. Anger throws poison into the system that no antibiotic can ever counteract.

Ten minutes of unbridled temper can waste enough strength for a half-day of wholesome work. Your physical energy is a gift from God, entrusted to you to be employed for His glory. It is a sin to take His gift and dissipate it through the trap doors of the emotional disposition.

Look not upon others and condemn them for jeopardizing their health by harmful habits and wasting energies on vain pursuits, while you yourself undermine your health by unworthy emotions, and take time—which by keeping your mind in an attitude of praise and faith could be constructively employed, instead you allow it to be a period of destructive action by entertaining such things as self-pity, remorse, and evil surmising.[6]

THE PATHWAY TO HEALING

The fundamental solution set forth in *Come Away, My Beloved* is "absolute confidence in [God's] loving care." That is the health prescription I am now pursuing in my own life. It strikes me as perfectly logical that someone who doesn't trust God, who allows herself to worry and fret and fuss, will get sick a lot more often than someone whose mind is kept in perfect peace, focusing on the goodness of God. That's just common sense—and it makes medical sense too. Is it a magic cure? Can it prevent all illness? Well, I don't know, but it's got to yield better results than the alternative.

The Bible says that meditating on God's Word can literally bring healing to our bodies. I urge you, even as I urge myself, to prayerfully consider the following passages:

6 Roberts, *Come Away, My Beloved*.

My son, do not forget my teaching,
    but keep my commands in your heart,
for they will prolong your life many years
    and bring you prosperity. (Proverbs 3:1–2)

My son, pay attention to what I say;
    listen closely to my words.
Do not let them out of your sight,
    keep them within your heart;
for they are life to those who find them
    and health to a man's whole body.
Above all else, guard your heart,
    for it is the wellspring of life. (Proverbs 4:20–23)

Remember, I am writing this as a woman who was sick for twenty years. I am not saying this from a position of strength but of brokenness. I am not quoting these verses "at you" in judgment. I am not advocating one brand of theology over another. (Quite the opposite: I'm sure I've given everyone something to bristle about!) I am sharing with you the answers I am pursuing in my own life: not a formula, not a magic potion for healing, but the pathway to healing.

The beautiful thing about Job—and for some reason, I had never paid much attention to this part of the story—is that in the end he finally gets "the life he signed up for." His suffering, while intense, represented only a very brief season in his life. His life was *not characterized* by suffering. He was showered with blessings, both before and after his trials. Suffering was *not* a way of life for Job; it was a valley he passed through. The Scripture says we may have to "walk through the valley of the shadow of death" (Psalm 23:4), but it doesn't say we have to build our homes there.

> *Suffering was not a way of life for Job; it was a valley he passed through.*

Perhaps you've heard people say, "The Lord has blessed me with good health." In so saying, I suspect God has also blessed them with a good, balanced perspective. It's a blessing I am eager to receive.

GROWTH GUIDE

Key Points to Remember

- Some Christians believe that suffering is inherently noble. As a result, they sometimes passively accept suffering that God never intended them to endure.
- It is clear from the book of Job that Satan has the power to afflict people with sickness and that God sometimes allows it. Nevertheless, the lives of God's favored children throughout the Old Testament were characterized by health and long life.
- Sometimes chronic illness draws us closer to God, but in many cases it causes people to become self-consumed.
- Jesus frequently healed sick people. He didn't go around making people sick so they could prove how much faith they had or merely to get their attention.
- Lack of faith is not the only explanation for the heartaches of life. It definitely explains some things, but not everything.
- The healthiest attitude toward sickness is to view it chiefly as the result of living in a fallen world, not primarily as being sent by God to make us holy or as a result of a lack of faith on our part.

- In many instances, sickness is nothing more than the logical consequence of our lifestyle. We don't always need to look for profound supernatural explanations when common sense will do.
- Medical science continues to confirm that many illnesses are rooted in emotional pain, which manifests itself in physical pain.
- God created us as triune beings: spirit, soul (mind, will, and emotions), and body. Whatever impacts one part of our being impacts the other two parts as well. If we neglect any area, the other two invariably suffer.
- The Bible says that meditating on God's Word can literally bring healing to our bodies.

Application Questions

1. Do you believe suffering is inherently noble? A sign that the sick person is a giant of the faith?

2. Have you ever been guilty of playing the martyr? Describe the impact on those around you.

3. In your personal experience, has sickness drawn you closer to God? Or has it made you more self-consumed?

4. In your observation of those around you, which of the two responses is most common among sick people (especially those who are chronically sick)?

5. Do you believe God inflicts or allows sickness in order to get someone's attention?

6. How much sickness, in your observation of family and friends, is nothing more than the logical consequences of lifestyle choices?

7. Many Christians neglect their body and then blame God or the devil when they get sick. Have you ever been guilty of doing that?

8. Have you been praying for healing while refusing to make the necessary lifestyle changes that might promote healing?

9. Do you know other people who have done this or perhaps routinely do it?

10. Is it possible that some of your physical suffering is rooted in emotional pain?

11. Again, from your own personal observation, how much physical suffering do you believe is rooted in emotional pain? Cite examples.

12. On a scale of 1 to 10 (1 being neglectful and 10 being extremely diligent), how well do you take care of your:

    _____ spirit

    _____ soul

    _____ body

13. Reread the extended passage from *Come Away, My Beloved*. What is your response?

14. Describe your own personal pathway to great health.

15. Consider undertaking a study of my book *Becoming the Woman I Want to Be: A 90-Day Journey to Renewing Spirit, Soul, and Body*.

Digging Deeper

- Read Psalm 6:
  What does the psalmist tell us about the health of his soul?

  What about the health of his body?

  Is the spiritual condition of the psalmist discernible?

  Are there connections between the health of his spirit, soul, and body?

- Meditate on Psalm 31:
  What circumstances is the psalmist facing?

How does he feel about them?

What about the condition of his spirit?

How about his body?

Does he tell us about the condition of his soul?

Again, what conclusions can you draw about the connections between spirit, soul, and body?

How do people treat him?

What does God do for him?

Do you really believe God will do those same things for you?

How does your life (the condition of your spirit, soul, and body) give evidence of your belief?

Look up the following verses and note what you find about health and healing:

Proverbs 3:7–8

Proverbs 4:20–22

Proverbs 12:18

Proverbs 15:4

Proverbs 15:30

Proverbs 16:24

Matthew 4:23

Matthew 9:35

Luke 6:19

Luke 9:10–11

3 John 1:2

Romans 12:1

Working It Into Your Life

1. Carefully evaluate the health of your body, soul, and spirit. Prayerfully consider whether you need to undertake a new diet or fitness regimen.
2. Go to a health food store and explore homeopathic remedies for some of your common ailments.
3. If you are chronically ill or just feeling sluggish, you might consider undertaking routine fasts to benefit your body and spirit. Begin with a twenty-four-hour fast, then a forty-eight-hour one, and perhaps build up to fasts of three, four, or even seven days. I once met a woman who fasted for forty days! Although I have not lost weight using the forty-eight-hour "diet juices," I have found them extremely beneficial during fasting—they prevent many of the common side effects, such as headaches and the jitters.

Rewrite One of This Week's Key Verses

_____

_____

_____

_____

_____

_____

Your Prayer in Response

_____

_____

_____

_____

_____

_____

_____

_____

_____

_____

*Heavenly Father, I know my health is a precious
gift from you. Please forgive me for treating the
temple of the Holy Spirit like a trash can! I know
my body is the only living sacrifice I have to
offer you, so I offer it to you right now. Empower
me to actively purify my life of anything that
contaminates my spirit, soul, or body, so that I can
glorify you. In Jesus' name. Amen.*

I signed up for love

CHAPTER EIGHT

I Signed Up for Love

My people have committed two sins: They have forsaken me, the spring of living water, and have dug their own cisterns, broken cisterns that cannot hold water.

Jeremiah 2:13

God likes my undivided attention.
    I like working out.
        We were at an impasse,
            Until the splat.

I can't think of any other word to adequately describe what happened on the treadmill that day.

S-P-L-A-T

For as long as I can remember, I've been obsessed with the size of my thighs. They don't seem to belong to me. I'm convinced they belong to someone else but have shown up and attached themselves just above my nice little calves. Now they are clinging to me like a lost child in a department store. I keep trying to tell them, "I am not your real mother. You better go find her." But they keep clinging. They stare back at me from every dressing room mirror. They wait for me each morning when I awake, defying me to conquer them.

Like many women, I have purchased every pill and potion that promised to serve as my ally in this all-important War on Thighs. I have tried every gadget and exercise scheme on the market. I have spent hours in the gym. I have consumed countless bottles of the 48-hour miracle diet guaranteed to take off ten pounds in a weekend. I even tried to enlist God's help by enrolling in a Christian weight-loss program. Hey, I was willing to put in the effort. It wasn't like I was sitting on the couch crying, "God, make me a salad with low-fat dressing and bring it in here." I was doing my part; he just needed to do his part to melt the fat away. But the thighs haven't budged an inch. No, not even an inch. Maybe you can relate!

Anyway, back to the *splat*. So there I was on the treadmill at the gym, running furiously, when I noticed that a friend of mine entered the room. I turned my head and called out to get her attention. I even attempted to convince her to run alongside me so we could "spur one another on toward love and good deeds." (See how scriptural I am?) Unfortunately, turning around was a bad move. I was distracted. And in a graceless moment of sheer humiliation, I fell flat on my face in the middle of the gym, right there in front of all those athletes with their firm bodies.

I could barely walk for the next few days. I had huge scabs

on my legs for weeks, and even now, many months later, the scars on my knees remain visible. The fall forced me to stop my frantic running, and in the process, I was also forced to confront the truth about what was going on inside of me. It was painful . . . but ultimately healing.

AM I LOVABLE?

A male friend recently asked me what all of the female obsession with body image was about. He failed to see the link between personal appearance and love. So I tried to explain it to him. It was one of those "men are from Mars" moments. He just couldn't see the connection! His exact words were, "What does working out at the gym have to do with LOVE?" In his mind, the perfect female body might grab a man's attention. But grabbing attention and getting love are two completely different things. Men understand that; women don't. That's why women do all kinds of crazy things to themselves in search of a man's love.

Grabbing attention and getting love are two completely different things.

Unfortunately, many of us are striving after an ideal that doesn't exist. When Michelle Pfeiffer appeared on the front cover of *Esquire* magazine a few years ago, countless women gazed at her photo and asked, "Why can't I look like her?" But the truth is Michelle Pfeiffer doesn't even look like that, at least not until the photo finishing company performs a little magic. Here's the invoice Scott Associates, Inc., of New York sent to *Esquire:*

- CLIENT: *Esquire*/T. Koppel
- PRODUCT: December Cover/Michelle Pfeiffer
- DESCRIPTION: Retouching 1 dye transfer two-piece strip of Michelle Pfeiffer in red dress. Clean up complexion, soften

eye lines, soften smile line, add color to lips, trim chin, remove neck lines, soften line under ear lobe, add highlights to earrings, add blush to cheek, clean up neck line, remove stray hair, remove hair strands on dress, adjust color and add hair on top of head, add dress on side to create better line, add dress on shoulder, clean up and smooth dress folds under arm and create one seam image on right side.

- TOTAL: $1,525.00[1]

The obsessive pursuit of perfection is not reasonable—and it will never bring us the love we desire.

And we wonder why WE don't look like the women on the covers of magazines! I do think God wants us to take reasonable care of our bodies. After all, it is the only living sacrifice we have to offer him, and the Scripture does say physical training is beneficial (Romans 12:1; 1 Corinthians 9:24–27; 1 Timothy 4:8). But the obsessive pursuit of perfection is not reasonable—and it will never bring us the love we desire.

At the end of the day it's not beauty and physical fitness that we really want. We want someone to love us. And we think that means we have to make ourselves lovable. But love isn't love if you have to earn it. Real love—God's love—is unconditional. He even loves women with cellulite. In fact, his Word says we are fearfully and wonderfully made, just the way we are. We don't need to change a thing to be lovable.

OF KIDS, FRIENDS, AND ANIMALS

I think what God wanted to say to me—and what I was finally able to hear once he had my undivided attention—is

---

[1] Duffy Robbins, *It's How You Play the Game* (Wheaton, IL: Scripture Press, 1991).

that there are different kinds of love. And I was pursuing the wrong kind. Around this time, my children and I were sitting on the couch one evening. Tara looked up from my lap and said, "Mommy, you're the bestest pillow in the world." I don't think she could have said that with as much conviction to a thin-thighed mommy. Your children no doubt would say the same of you.

And I know you have girl friends who love you to pieces, even when you can't fit into the size you'd like to wear. I suspect some of them may actually like you better with a little meat on your bones.

If you happen to have a dog, you've probably noticed how much he or she loves you. Even when you haven't brushed your teeth or combed your hair, your dog is still happy to see you. When I come home from a trip to the grocery store, my dogs are so excited you'd think I was returning from a tour around the world. My chickens and goats seem fond of me too. Some might say it's just because I feed them. Nevertheless, lately I'm finding great delight in how happy they are to see me, despite my physical shortcomings. Our donkey doesn't care for me, but you can't win them all, can you?

THE BUCKET LADY

I'd like to write a book called *Confessions of a Recovering Bucket Lady*, but my publisher is afraid no one would know what it was about. So let me tell you so you'll know in advance. When the book comes out, I'm sure you'll rush out to buy your copy. At least that's what I plan to tell my publisher.

I firmly believe God deliberately designed all human beings with a hole in their heart the size of the Grand Canyon. It's what Blaise Pascal is credited with calling "the God-shaped void"—a place that can only be filled through a personal relationship with our Creator. All of us sense that emptiness within, and we are driven to fill it. But rather than turning to God for fulfillment, as we should, many of us run everywhere else instead. We go out into the world with our little clamoring bucket, and we hand it to the people around us and say, "Fill me. Fix me. Love me. Make me feel OK." We turn to our parents, our husband, our children, our friends, our church, our career, expecting them to be to us what only God can be. The result is what I've termed the Bucket Lady Syndrome.

The Bucket Lady always thinks the answer to her emptiness is right around the next corner. So she tries to get her bucket filled with accomplishments—both personal and professional. She tries to fill it with the perfect house and the perfect circle of friends. The Bucket Lady might even look good, because she's just got to have great clothes, the right hairstyle and makeup. She's busy at church, trying to fill her bucket with Christian rituals and church busywork. The reality is she will never rest until that hole is filled—and it can never be filled with what's in that bucket.

Jeremiah 2:13 puts it this way: "My people have committed two sins. They have forsaken me, the spring of living water, and have dug their own cisterns, broken cisterns that cannot hold water." The Bucket Lady tries to fill her life with things that can never satisfy.

Now, I'm going to tell you the truth. And if you can get past the fact that it might hurt your feelings, I think you can get set free in a big way before this chapter is through. First, I want to acknowledge that it's entirely possible for you to have people in your life that couldn't care less about you. You hand them the bucket and they toss it aside. But the painful truth is you are probably surrounded by people who are bailing and bailing just as fast as they can. But they are never going to fill that hole. *Never.*

I got an e-mail the other day from a woman who had heard me speak recently and was ready to retire as her mother's bailer.[2] (Your bailer is the person you expect to bail and bail until you get your fill.) She said her entire childhood was devoted to filling her mother's bucket: getting straight A's, being the star of the school play, becoming a cheerleader and class president, etc. Then she worked hard to get into a prestigious university so her mom would have bragging rights. When she graduated, she landed a high-profile, high-paying job and lavished her mom with gifts. She literally drove herself to physical collapse trying to make her mom proud. Trying to fill her mother's bucket. Of course, it was never enough. Her mom was the same unhappy person. She was just an unhappy person with a lot to brag about.

Who do you expect to be your bailer? Let me give you some clues: Who has the ability to make you angrier than anyone else? Who has the power to disappoint you most profoundly? That's your bailer.

Who do you like to brag about? That's your bailer too.

My ministry is to women, but whenever I speak, there's invariably a man or two milling about, running the sound system or organizing the food service. I'll never forget walking out of a conference late one Friday night and hearing a male voice behind me. I turned around and there was this six-foot-something man with tears streaming down his face. "Can I help you?" I asked.

"That woman you were talking about in there? The Bucket Lady? That's my wife. I love her, but she's killing me. No matter what I do for that woman, it's never enough."

---

[2] I know that "to bail" normally means to remove water from a boat, but in this case we mean someone who attempts to save or "bail" someone out.

Wow!

If your husband had the opportunity, and the courage, to follow me out the door, do you think we'd have the same conversation? It's something to ponder anyway.

Sometimes we women tend to think men aren't quite as smart as we are. Let me tell you, your husband might be a whole lot smarter than you think. Maybe he's spent years and years trying to fill your bucket. But he figured out, long before YOU did, that he was never going to fill that giant chasm in your heart. So he put down the bucket . . . and picked up the remote.

The next time you see your husband staring blankly at the television, just remind yourself: "That's one real smart cookie sitting there."

Here's another clue: If your husband would rather be anywhere else, doing anything else other than be with you, you're probably a Bucket Lady. (Then again, maybe you just married a jerk. But promise me you'll pray about it.)

Will you be smart enough to let your husband off the hook? To let him officially retire as your bailer? Maybe you could buy him a gold watch and host a special ceremony. I'll bet when you stop expecting him to fill you, he might come out of hiding. Then again, he might stay hidden behind that remote—or newspaper, or office work, or golf game—forever. That's okay. You don't need him to fill you anymore.

And I'll tell the single ladies a little secret. Men are born with an internal Bucket Lady Detection Device. They see a Bucket Lady coming at them—I mean a woman who's just trying way too hard to get their attention and win their love—and something inside them starts screaming, "Run for your life! Run for your life!" Now, they might dally with you before they run for the hills. But you can take it to the bank: He won't stick around long enough to fill your bucket. And he might just reach into your heart, pull out what little you've got, and leave you dry.

No doubt you remember the story of the Samaritan woman who meets Jesus at the well. (If not, read John 4:4–43.) This Bucket Lady had had five husbands, plus she was living with a guy, and we can just imagine how many boyfriends were thrown into the mix. Talk about "lookin' for love in all the wrong places, lookin' for love on too many faces"! Now you would think, if it were possible for a man to fill a woman's bucket, one of these men could have gotten it right if only *by accident*. I mean, at some point, wouldn't the law of averages have to work in her favor?

The problem is it's not possible.

So she meets up with Jesus. And he tells her the same thing he tells the rest of us: "Everyone who drinks this water will be thirsty again, but whoever drinks the water I give him will never thirst. Indeed, the water I give him will become in him a spring of water welling up to eternal life" (John 4:13–14).

Then the story includes a fascinating little detail: "Then, leaving her water jar . . ." (v. 28).

Did you catch that?

She left her bucket at the well!

Once she allowed Jesus to fill that hole in her heart, to place within her that spring of water welling up to eternal life, she didn't need her bucket anymore. She didn't have to live like a Bucket Lady anymore.

You don't have to live like a Bucket Lady anymore either.

You don't have to live like a Bucket Lady anymore.

LAVISHED BY HIS LOVE

If we were together at a conference right now, I would invite you forward for the "Bucket Surrendering Ceremony." But you can participate right where you are, in your own heart and mind. I want you to bring to mind a picture of your bailer—that person you expect to fill the emptiness inside of you. That person who has the power to make you angrier than anyone else; the person who can disappoint you most profoundly. Or maybe it's the person you like to brag about. Get a clear picture of that person in your mind. Now imagine him/her standing there with your little bucket in hand, scooping and pouring furiously. Now I want you to imagine yourself reaching toward this person and taking back your bucket. Ask his forgiveness and tell him you are letting him off the hook. He (or she) no longer has to keep you satisfied.

Now I want you to picture yourself with your little bucket walking toward the well where Jesus is seated. Kneel down at his feet. Ask him to fill you to overflowing with the Living Water of the Holy Spirit. Ask him to so lavish you with his love, his approval, his acceptance that you no longer need to frantically search for love, approval, and acceptance from people. Imagine yourself handing him your bucket and leaving it safely in his care.

You won't need it anymore.

You can return to the well as often as you like. I go there every morning and drink deeply of God's unlimited reservoir of love and acceptance. That's why I describe myself as "in recovery." For some of us, the escape from the Bucket Lady Syndrome will be a day-by-day, moment-by-moment way of life. This is my prayer for you:

> I pray that out of his glorious riches he may strengthen you
> with power through his Spirit in your inner being, so that Christ

may dwell in your hearts through faith. And I pray that you, being rooted and established in love, may have power, together with all the saints, to grasp how wide and long and high and deep is the love of Christ, and to know this love that surpasses knowledge—that you may be filled to the measure of all the fullness of God. (Ephesians 3:16–19)

The amazing thing is once you allow God to fill you, something beautiful begins to happen. Not only are you officially a *Recovering* Bucket Lady, who no longer needs people to fill her, you can be one of those rare gems who has something genuinely worthwhile to offer the world. You'll have the love of God shed abroad in your heart, overflowing toward everyone you meet.

Suddenly ministry won't be something you have to add to your list of things to do. It will just be who you are. All you'll have to do is walk into the room, and people will be blessed because you came.

And if that isn't the life you signed up for, I don't know what is.

GROWTH GUIDE

Key Points to Remember

- God wants us to take reasonable care of our bodies, but the obsessive pursuit of perfection is not reasonable—and it will never bring us the love we desire.
- God says you are lovable exactly the way you are; you don't have to change a thing to earn his love and attention.
- God designed all of us with a hole in our hearts the size of the Grand Canyon so we would be driven to him to fill us. Unfortunately, we run everywhere else to be filled—and turn into a Bucket Lady in the process.

- We go out into the world with our little bucket and expect people to fill us, fix us, love us, and make us feel okay. We fail to realize it is impossible to fill a hole the size of the Grand Canyon with a bucketful of anything.

- You can determine who you expect to fill you by asking yourself: Who can make me angrier than anyone else? Who can disappoint me most profoundly? Who do I like to brag about?

- Many men figure out before their wives do that they will never be able to fill that empty place inside the women they love, so they put down the bucket and pick up the remote!

- The Bible tells us that after the Samaritan woman allowed Jesus to give her the Living Water, she left her jar at the well. She didn't have to be a Bucket Lady anymore.

- When you allow the Living Water to fill those empty places in your heart, you won't have to be a Bucket Lady anymore either.

- Once you've surrendered your bucket, you can be one of those rare gems who has something genuinely worthwhile to offer the world. You'll have the love of God shed abroad in your heart, overflowing toward everyone you meet.

Application Questions

1. How do you feel about your body?

2. Is there one part of your body that drives you nuts? What is it? To what lengths have you gone to try to change it?

3. Have you been through a "midlife crisis"? What's the craziest thing you did during that time?

4. Do you take reasonable care of your body?

5. Are you now—or have you ever been—obsessed with the pursuit of perfection? What were the results?

6. Have you ever felt desperate to win male attention? What did that desperation drive you to do?

7. Which kind of love are you seeking?

8. What type of love is most meaningful in your life right now? Who provides that love? Describe.

9. Have you ever sensed God seeking you? When? What was your response?

10. Are you a Bucket Lady? Who do you expect to bail for you?

11. How has that affected your relationship?

12. How would your relationship be different if you released your bailer?

Digging Deeper

- Read John 15:9–17:

  This was the last opportunity Jesus had to teach his disciples in depth. What subject did he choose to speak about?

What does that tell you about how important this subject is to Jesus?

WHY does he want us to love one another? What will be the result in our own lives when we love others?

- Read Ephesians 3:14–21:
  List all the things Paul prayed for his friends:

  What are we to be rooted and established in?

  If you were instructing someone how to be filled with love, based on this passage, what would you say?

- Meditate on Psalm 16, especially verses 9–11:
  Who fills the psalmist?

  What is he filled with?

  How does that filling affect his heart?

  His tongue?

  His body?

Look up the following Scriptures and note what you discover about love and what we are to be filled with:

John 1:15–16

John 13:34

John 15:9–17

Romans 5:5

Romans 12:9–10

Romans 13:8–10

1 Corinthians 2:9–10

1 Corinthians 13:1–13

1 Peter 1:22

1 John 4:7–12

1 John 4:16–21

Working It Into Your Life

1. Write love letters to important people in your life: husband, parents, children, friends.
2. Have your own Bucket Surrendering Ceremony as described in the lesson.
3. Hold a retirement ceremony for your bailer. Take that person out for a special dinner (or prepare one) and present him or her with a gift to symbolize the retirement.

Rewrite One of This Week's Key Verses

_____

_____

_____

_____

_____

_____

Your Prayer in Response

_____

_____

_____

_____

_____

_____

_____

_____

_____

_____

Heavenly Father, I thank you for loving me so much
that you sent your only Son to die on a cross for me. I
pray that the Holy Spirit would so fill my heart with
love that I would have something to give to others.
Help me, Lord, not to be a Bucket Lady—one who
desperately seeks love and approval from others.
Help me instead to be filled with joy in your presence.
Jesus, thank you for showing us how to love and
for setting an example by laying down your life for
us. I want to learn to lay my life down—my needs
and concerns—so that I can focus on the needs and
concerns of others. Amen.

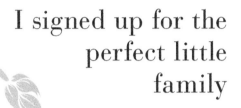

I signed up for the
perfect little
family

CHAPTER NINE

I Signed Up for the Perfect Little Family

Blessed is the [woman] who fears the Lord,
who finds great delight in his commands.
[Her] children will be mighty in the land;
the generation of the upright will be blessed.

Psalm 112:1–2

My daughter Leah is fascinated by the workings of the universe. It's not unusual for me to find her sitting by the window at night, just staring up at the sky. Earlier this year, she had a school assignment to write *one paragraph* about the planets. She wrote *seven pages* before I told her she had to stop. She then proceeded to draw an elaborate cover for her "report." So you've got the idea, right? Leah loves the night sky.

A few years ago, Comet Tempel-Tuttle swung past the sun for the first time in nearly thirty-five years, creating an unusually active Leonid meteor shower. But Leah and I didn't get to watch the meteor shower together because it happened on the weekend. And she is with her father on weekends. I called her late in the evening and reminded her to set the alarm clock for 2:00 AM, just as I was setting mine. I told her I'd call first thing in the morning and we could tell each other how many shooting stars we had counted.

The meteor show was spectacular. As I lay on a blanket in the middle of the night—without Leah by my side—I comforted myself by singing the old Disney tune "Somewhere out there beneath the pale moonlight, someone's thinking of me and loving me tonight." (Do you remember it? Sung by Linda Ronstadt?) It was bittersweet.

The next morning was pure bitterness. I called Leah, and the moment she heard my voice, she started sobbing. Her dad was groggy when the alarm went off . . . so he turned it off.

She had missed the meteor shower.

Perhaps that seems like a small thing. And I guess that's what broke my heart. I didn't want a vacation on the French Riviera. I was just an ordinary mom who wanted to share a meteor shower with my daughter. Was that really asking so much?

When I was expecting my first child, I had the same dreams every new mother has. I never dreamed I would be robbed of such a simple pleasure. I remember when I decided to home-school. I was so excited I read every book on the market. Then I reread them. Every Monday night I gathered together with a group of homeschooling moms. We called ourselves "The Charlotte Mason Society." We were going to shelter and protect our children. We signed up for double duty, as both mother and teacher, but we knew it would be worth all the sacrifices. Because we were going to spare them the heartaches we had endured.

I bought dozens of teaching tapes by homeschooling experts and listened to them over and over and over. In my car. In the kitchen. While I went for my daily walk. I attended conferences. Everyone told me the same thing. If I would just sign up for homeschooling, I could have the perfect little family. My kids wouldn't become "worldly," they wouldn't become "secular humanists," they wouldn't go through teenage rebellion. I might even be able to get them to wear matching outfits.

I signed up to have the perfect little family. I did more than sign up, though. I gave it everything I had to give. A neighbor once said to me, "Donna, I've never met anyone who tries as hard as you." My mom tells me the same thing all the time, except she's usually crying when she says it. We even moved our family to a homestead in the mountains, seeking a simpler way of life. I sincerely thought we had a chance to make the cover of *Perfect Homeschooling Family* magazine.

But something went wrong. Terribly wrong.

I won't tell you the whole story, but believe me, it was a nightmare. An absolute nightmare. I didn't sign up for it. Now I'm just trying to get past it, by the grace and mercy of God.

So here I am. Trying to piece my little family back together. A patchwork of Mom's house, Dad's house, and heartache like you wouldn't believe. Well, maybe you would believe it. Maybe you've lived through far worse. Divorce is hell. Don't let anyone convince you otherwise. Having said that let me add a sentence that will blow plenty of people out of the water: Nothing has made me more like Jesus than my divorce. More compassionate. Less inclined to throw stones.

Don't get me wrong. I didn't sign up for divorce and I'm not glad it happened. Having witnessed the excruciating pain my children have endured, I know why God says, "I hate divorce" (Malachi 2:16). We should all hate it. Experts say the pain experienced by children of divorce actually gets *worse* over time. Hard to imagine, but from where I sit, it sure looks to be true.

I always tell people, if there is any conceivable way to save your marriage, if there is even a shred of love or respect left between you, by all means, stay together for the sake of the children. Get on your knees and beg God for the grace to make the most of whatever you have to work with.

For my part, I keep adding animals, thinking that will alleviate the pain. If not the pain, then at least the loneliness. I was always appalled when I went to someone's house and discovered they allowed a dog indoors. Unthinkable! Guess who now has a German shepherd sleeping in her bedroom? Not only do I feel safer, I'm grateful for the company.

Leah worked all last summer to buy a miniature donkey named Brighty. He served as a great distraction for a while. The empty-nesters who live nearby "gave" Leah a horse: a twenty-two-year-old Arabian-Tennessee Walker named Frisco. Frisco still lives with the Morris family, but he's Leah's horse, and she can ride him whenever she likes. Some days she spends more time over there than over here. I can't say I blame her. Home is a constant reminder of what we've lost.

We're not alone, of course. According to noted Christian psychologist Dr. Neil Clark Warren, "Seventy percent of us have experienced a broken home either from our parents' or our own failed marriages."[1] So much for the perfect little families we all signed up for.

---

[1] Candy Williams, "Psychologist Offers Help in Finding Your Soul Mate," *The Tribune-Review*, February 12, 2002.

Which reminds me of an e-mail Tracie Peterson[2] sent me not long ago. She said (I'm paraphrasing here), "Donna, sometimes life is like this. You're walking a narrow path between two walls. Straight ahead is a huge pile of horse manure. What are you going to do? Turn around? Pretend you don't notice the manure? Deny that it's there? Or are you going to press on through, knowing full well how bad it stinks, so you can get to the other side?"

Jesus is taking you to green pastures, right beside the still waters.

Tracie thought I should press on through. And she thought it might be helpful for me to stand up and say, in a really loud voice: "There are a whole lot of wonderful Christians—people who love the Lord with everything they've got, people who never signed up for horse manure—walking between these two walls." So hold your nose and press on through. If people point out that you've got horse manure on your shoes, tell them you're going to keep walking forward with Jesus until the smell goes away. He's taking you to green pastures, right beside the still waters, and that ought to solve the problem. Then tell them you're praying they don't get stuck between those two walls.

NOT ALWAYS WHAT IT SEEMS

It hasn't escaped my kids' notice that our lives have changed dramatically since the divorce. For one thing, matching outfits have entirely lost their appeal for me. I still homeschool, but I canceled my subscription to *Perfect Homeschooling Family* magazine and stopped reading books and listening to tapes that promised A+B would always equal C. I did A+B but I ended up

---

[2] Bestselling author of Christian fiction.

Life doesn't always fit into nice, neat little formulas.

with a great big F anyway. Life doesn't always fit into nice, neat little formulas. Bummer. 'Cause I'm quite certain C would have been preferable to F.

My children and I still pine for the good ol' days, even though deep in our hearts we all know it was pretty much the bad ol' days, glossed over with some good acting on Mom's part. Sometimes we struggle with envy when we look around and see other people with their seemingly perfect little families.

We were in the car one day when I asked Leah why she hadn't played with Rachel lately. She said she felt weird because Rachel couldn't relate to all the problems we were facing. "Her life is perfect. She's so lucky!" Leah declared.

I couldn't believe what I was hearing. "Don't you know what she's lived through? Doesn't she talk about it?"

"Talk about what, Mom?"

Let me back up and tell you about Rachel's family, the Cunninghams, because they are among my all-time favorite families. Her parents, Dave and Melanie, have a great marriage. Dave treats Melanie like a queen, and she is truly one of the most sweet-spirited, godly women I've ever known. And I say that knowing her very, very well and having watched her closely in stressful situations. I met them and their two beautiful daughters at a homeschool gathering several years ago. My first thought was, *Now, there's a family who wouldn't know a problem if it walked up and introduced itself.* They looked like they'd just stepped off the pages of *Little House on the Prairie.*

Several years passed before I found out just how wrong I was. When I discovered the truth, I was initially stunned. But then, it simply reinforced what I've always known: No one knows what

214

people are up against in their private world. That's why we're completely unqualified to pass judgments.

Holding on to your seat? This is the THIRD marriage for both Dave and Melanie. Not second. Third. You'd never guess it, but Dave is not their children's "real" father; their "real" father is missing in action and has been throughout most of the children's lives.

Shortly before their marriage eight years ago, Dave and Melanie both encountered Jesus in a life-changing way. After years spent wandering lost in the wilderness, they'd finally found the way home. They were thrilled about their new life with God and each other. At last they had discovered the life they originally signed up for.

Not quite.

Within a year of his conversion, Dave's prior life caught up with him. He had committed a white-collar crime, and although he was a new man with a new life, he had to pay the price. So he was sent to federal prison. Dave says it was the best five months of his life, even though it was the worst five months of his life. It forced him to get on his knees. It forced him to confront the truth about his life, like how he'd inadvertently signed up for most of his heartache through his own foolish choices (see chapter 4). We reap what we sow, forgiveness notwithstanding. It gave him ample time to study his brand-new Bible and to discover that God is far more interested in what's going on inside of us than what's going on around us.

The Cunninghams also found out who their real friends were. Like Mildred, an older woman at the little Baptist church they attend. The first week Dave was in prison, she took out a piece of paper during Sunday school and passed it around for everyone to write him a note of encouragement. She did that every week without fail. A man from their church called Melanie every single day—yes, every single day—to ask if there was anything he or his wife could do to help.

Doesn't it do your heart good when the church gets it right?

The Cunninghams learned a valuable lesson

God can heal and transform a patchwork family. He is our Redeemer!

very early in their Christian walk: not to worry about "what the neighbors will say" but rather "fix your eyes on Jesus, the author and perfecter of your faith" (Hebrews 12:2). They learned to focus on keeping their hearts right before God and to let God handle their circumstances. They knew God was doing a mighty work inside their family, even though it looked like a mess from the outside. Eventually, the inward reality manifested itself to a watching world. As one of those watching, let me tell you, it's beautiful to behold. It gives me hope, knowing God can heal and transform a patchwork family. He is our Redeemer!

THE SHOW MUST GO ON

Many of us get it backward. We ignore the internal reality and focus on outward performance. We're more interested in what the neighbors think than what God thinks. So we push and shove our families around, trying to fit them into a particular mold. I've been guilty of it myself. I'll never forget what I said to my two daughters on Mother's Day several years ago.

I said: "IT'S M-O-T-H-E-R'S D-A-A-A-Y!"

It's all in the tone of voice, don't you know?

You see, I wanted them to dress up in matching outfits, put matching smiles on their faces, and look adorable at church. I wanted them to "rise up and call me blessed" in such a way that the whole world joined the chorus. At my seminars, I do this funny little skit about Sunday mornings. Maybe you can relate. Let's pretend it's Sunday morning at your house. You hit the snooze button five times, so when you finally roll out of bed, you realize you're going to be late for church. Now, there's a woman who stands in the back of the sanctuary, making a note of everyone who can't get to church on time. You're not gonna end up on her list! I don't think so!

So you leap to your feet and run into your first grader's room. "Wake up, Katie," you say with sweet urgency. "Time to get up for church. Don't forget to bring your Bible. Because you know, every time you bring your Bible, you get two Bible bucks. And once you get ten Bible bucks, you get a star on the chart. And I couldn't help but notice that you're falling behind Jenny on the star chart. Let's get going!"

Okay, that went well. Now the frightening part: You have to enter your teenager's room. "Kristi, Kristi, wake up, honey. We're going to be late for church! Hurry up!" She looks at you as through a glass darkly, then scowls. You remember last night's screaming match. Uh-oh. Better make amends quickly. "Listen, Kristi, I know I really lost it over that whole belly-button piercing deal. I shouldn't have said such mean things to you. But listen. Just last week at Sunday school, the Joneses were talking about the sin of body piercing. Now, you know your dad is up for elder! Do you know how many casseroles I've had to cook to get him on the elder board? If people find out our kids are piercing body parts, it could blow the whole deal. Now, cover that up and let's get going!"

Everyone runs around like lunatics, snapping at each other all the while. Then you jump into the car and race to church, cutting people off along the way. "Hey, get out of my way! I'm late for church!" (Of course, what really bugs me is what happens *after* church. Everyone goes out for lunch, prays before the meal with great fanfare—then makes the poor waiter SPLIT THE CHECK. Ugh! I think we could turn the tide in this country if Christians would do their own math in restaurants. But I digress!)

Finally you make it into the church parking lot. Mom reminds everyone: "Smiles on our faces. This is church." You get out of the car, and behold, the head of the elder board approaches. Mom does her little beauty-pageant wave and says sweetly, "Praise the Lord. You know, this morning in our family devotional time . . ."

Well, you get the idea. It's all about smiling and lying. And we wonder why our kids drop out of church. Who would have guessed?

T. S. Eliot observed, "The last temptation is the final treason: to do the right thing for the wrong reason."[3] If he's right, and I happen to think he is, there are a whole lot of nice polite church ladies out there committing the final treason.

It's not what you do but why you do it that counts.

It's not what you do but why you do it that counts.

Again, it's not what you do but why you do it that counts.

It's not what the neighbors *think* is true about your family that matters; it's what your children *know* is true about your family that matters. Even more important than your children's opinion, however, is God's opinion. God looks at your heart. That's either good news or bad news, depending upon how you're living your life. I encourage you—even as I remind myself—to live your life before an Audience of One.

Another one of my favorite passages is 1 Corinthians 4:2–5:

---

[3] From his play *Murder in the Cathedral* (1935).

Now it is required that those who have been given a trust must prove faithful. I care very little if I am judged by you or by any human court; indeed, I do not even judge myself. My conscience is clear, but that does not make me innocent. It is the Lord who judges me. Therefore judge nothing before the appointed time; wait till the Lord comes. He will bring to light what is hidden in darkness and will expose the motives of men's hearts. At that time each will receive his praise from God.

God knows our motives and he will reward us according to what is in our heart, not based upon how well we perform. What would it profit a woman to fool the whole world, smiling and lying the whole way, when her heart isn't right before God? And why should it matter to a woman if the whole world misunderstands her, misjudges her, underestimates her, if her heart is right before God?

> *God knows our motives and he will reward us according to what is in our heart, not based upon how well we perform.*

GETTING WITH THE PROGRAM

Maybe you're thinking, "Hey, wait a minute, Donna. You're being too hard on us moms. We just want what's best for our kids." On one level, I'm certain that is absolutely true. On a deeper level, I'm not so sure. If we really want what's best for our kids, we'll ask God to show us. And I can't imagine God instructing people to push their kids the way I routinely see parents pushing their kids. I could be wrong, of course, but in this particular case, I don't think I am.

I recently read a magazine article about how obsessed Americans are with kids' sports. One particular sentence caught my attention. It said: "The Cold War is over . . . and the East

Germans won." Think about it. It applies to many areas, not just sports.

You may think you're just trying to be a good parent, but I'm challenging you to look deeper to see if something else is going on. You're just trying to get little Bobby to soccer practice. Just trying to help Susie get an A on her paper. Just trying to get the family to church on time. But they refuse to get with the program. This may sound unimaginable, but maybe your kids aren't the ones standing in the way of your progress. Maybe God is and he's using your kids as a roadblock. (Read Numbers 22:4–33 and think about who was really blocking Balaam's path.) Maybe God doesn't want you to get to soccer, softball, gymnastics, and band practice on time. Maybe he doesn't want your kids to "get with the program," and that's why their hearts aren't in it.

You know the program I'm talking about. The one where we push little Jason into the right preschool so he can learn to read early and get a head start so he can do well in grade school so they'll put him in all the advanced classes in high school so everyone will know "what a marvelous job we've done with him." Meanwhile, we want him to excel in sports so he can make the varsity team and catch the attention of college scouts so he can get into a top-notch university so he can get a great job so he can live in a beautiful house and buy nice things so he can die with a lot of stuff.

THE BUCKET LADY REVISITED

In a very real sense, it all comes back to the Bucket Lady desperately trying to find someone or something to validate her existence. We feel like we need to justify ourselves and give the world a good reason why it should allow us to take up breathing space on the planet. If only we could "accomplish" something! (More on that in the final chapter.) Our society is obsessed with success, but we're not sure how, as women, we can measure it. I don't meet many women who are still trying to break through the glass ceiling, although I assume they're still out there. But I know many women are working outside their homes just so they can buy more stuff. Of course, that's not the only reason women work outside the home. Some do because God has called them to a particular career or ministry; others because they can't survive on one income; still others because they are single parents. But I think ya'll know what I'm talking about.

Some women seek a sense of accomplishment and validation through ministry or charity involvement. I've talked with many church leaders, and they are unanimous in concurring with my assessment that one of the major problems in your average church is people entering into ministry for the wrong reasons. They aren't in ministry to serve but to get their bucket filled. Why? Because they are not allowing God to fill it and—this is so key—they've given up hope of getting it filled at home. So they run to church with their empty, clamoring buckets. The results are both predictable and inevitable.

My guess is, however, most women reading this book define success according to their relationships. It is said, "Behind every successful man there is a _____ woman." You can fill in the blank based on whatever kind of woman you think it takes. So if your husband is successful, you are successful. Does it follow, then, that if your husband is a failure (however you want to define that), you are a failure?

I've had the unfortunate displeasure of meeting women who brag incessantly about their husbands. As I'm sure you've noticed, there's a difference between loving admiration and bragging. It's subtle but unmistakable. During the Gulf War, there was a woman in our neighborhood you couldn't get within a mile of without hearing how her husband was single-handedly making the world safe for democracy. I remember one occasion where she waxed eloquent about her heroic husband—and how he was her ticket to the good life—for nearly an hour. It wouldn't have been too dreadful except there were two widows and three divorced women in the room. Maybe she was just proud of her husband, but I suspect something else was going on. It was her way of saying, "I may not seem wonderful, but imagine how wonderful I must be if *such* a man loves me."

If you're constantly goading your husband on to success, you might stop and ask yourself, why? Why is it so important for him to climb higher and higher, earning more and more money? Is it about him? Or is it about you?

Far more common than women bragging about their husbands is women bragging about their kids. What's that about? Maybe it's about a lot of things, and I don't pretend to know the motives of every bragging mom in the world. But I do think there's tremendous pressure on Christian women to make their kids turn out right. I've felt the pressure; I've given in to the pressure.

Is there something inherently wicked about kids playing soccer? Of course not! The question, again, isn't "What are you doing?" but "Why are you doing it?" If you take your kids to soccer practice because their bodies are the temple of the Holy Spirit and need to be exercised, that's wonderful. Or because they love playing soccer, that's wonderful. If you're doing it because Doreen's kids are playing soccer or because your child has a chance at a soccer scholarship, maybe you need to think twice about it.

THE BLESSING ISN'T FOR SALE

Have I left you wondering, "Doesn't anybody get it right? Doesn't anyone have the perfect little family we all signed up for?" Actually, I have seen a few, but they are NOT first generation Christians.[4] They are almost invariably people who were raised in genuine Christian homes—as opposed to "smiling and lying" Christian homes—where a premium was placed on loving God and loving people. Often they represent many generations of devout believers.

I'll never forget sharing the platform with a beautiful young woman who gave her testimony and sang just before I was scheduled to speak. Typically, she spoke to teenage girls, but this was a group comprised mostly of women in their thirties and beyond. However, she did not alter her message to suit the audience, which was initially very unfortunate—but ultimately powerful.

She shared about her life growing up in an incredibly warm, loving Christian home—how her father always cherished her and how easy that made it for her to embrace the love of a heavenly Father. She told about a special dinner date she had with her father, early in her teen years, and how she pledged to save herself for marriage. She committed herself never even to date in the traditional sense but to hold out for God's perfect choice.

And because she chose not to waste her time on the dating scene, she was able to focus on her studies and gain admittance to a prestigious university. Her unspoiled beauty and purity won the attention of the judges at the Miss America pageant, where she was a finalist. God gifted her with an extraordinary singing

---

[4] For more on the topic of first generation Christians, please refer to my book *Standing Firm* (Bethany House, 2001).

voice, and because she was faithful to cultivate that gift and use it for his glory, she recorded a nationally released CD before turning twenty-two.

Shortly thereafter, God did indeed reward her faithfulness by bringing along a handsome, wealthy professional athlete from a wonderful Christian home who fell madly in love with her. When she shared the story of his marriage proposal, it was like something out of a fairy tale. He sang to her at the wedding, and he too had such an extraordinary voice that a music company executive, who was on hand for the ceremony, offered him a contract on the spot.

In between these amazing stories of God's abundant blessings, she sang like an angel. When the women finally realized "the other shoe" was never going to drop, many of them were visibly shaken. The brightness and beauty of her life in contrast to the darkness they had endured was overwhelming. When she finished, the pain in the audience was palpable. I begged God to give me a word for these women. And did he ever! I picked up the microphone and simply said, "Someday, I want my granddaughter to stand on a stage and tell that *exact same story*. Don't you?"

The audience thundered.

They suddenly got it.

This beautiful young woman's life story was not a message for them; it was a message for their descendants. It was not a word concerning what their lives *should have been* but what their descendants' lives *could be*.

Did you know the Bible says blessings pass from generation to generation? Look:

> I, the Lord your God, am a jealous God, punishing the children for the sin of the fathers to the third and fourth generation of those who hate me, but showing love to a thousand generations

of those who love me and keep my commandments. (Exodus 20:5–6)

A thousand generations? A thousand generations! I'm not one to shout "Hallelujah," but here it comes: H-A-L-L-E-L-U-J-A-H! I've got a promise from the God of the universe right there in black and white. He says he will show love to a thousand generations of my children if I love him and keep his commands.

Wow. That works for me!

I believe God showed me something very powerful about my family and the spiritual heritage he is calling me to labor toward—not for me, not for the neighbors—for my children:

Blessed is the [woman] who fears the Lord,
who finds great delight in his commands.
[Her] children will be mighty in the land;
the generation of the upright will be blessed.
(Psalm 112:1–2)

Here's what God spoke to my heart: "You thought you could buy my blessing with a formula. With your A+B=C. You thought you could get what 'they' got if you worked hard enough and wrestled with me long enough. My blessing is not for sale, and it can't be demanded from me. It is a gift. A gift I give to your children as a reward for your obedience." I have finally come to grips with the fact that I will never personally experience the life I signed up for. There's already been too much heartache for me. But I believe my children—and especially my grandchildren—will be mighty in the land. They will tell stories of God's abundant blessings that will make people tremble. That awareness sets me far down the road to hope and healing!

It's not exactly what I signed up for . . . but I'll take it!

GROWTH GUIDE

Key Points to Remember

- Most Christian books on family life promise that A+B=C; that is, if you do certain things, you are guaranteed certain results. However, some people do A+B but get an F anyway.

- When you face a family crisis, focus on keeping your heart right before God, and let him handle your circumstances.

- Don't worry about what the neighbors say about your family; fix your eyes on Jesus and let him transform you from the inside out.

- When we are more interested in what the neighbors think than what God thinks, we push and shove our families around, trying to fit them into a particular mold.

- It's not what the neighbors *think* is true about your family that matters; it's what your children *know* is true about your family that matters.

- God knows our motives, and he will reward us according to what is in our heart, not based upon how well we perform. Live your life before an Audience of One.

- Most women define their success according to their relationships: If their husband is successful and their children accomplish a lot, they feel successful. Otherwise, they feel like failures.

- God's blessing is not for sale and it can't be obtained through working a formula. It is a gift he gives to our children as a reward for our obedience.

Application Questions

1. Have you ever missed an important event in your child's life? How did that make you feel?

2. Before you had children, no doubt you dreamed of the perfect little family. Describe what you had in mind.

3. How does the reality compare with your dream?

4. Do you notice a disparity between the way Christian family experts say your life "should" be and the way it really is? How do you account for that?

5. Are you among the 70 percent of the population affected by divorce? How has it affected you?

6. Have you ever faced a family crisis that taught you who your real friends were? What did you learn from that experience?

7. Are you more focused on outward performance or inward reality? What evidence can you give to support your answer?

8. Have you ever been guilty of pushing and shoving your family into a particular mold in an effort to impress other people?

9. Could you relate to the "Sunday morning" skit?

10. Is there any aspect of your approach to the Christian life that might be driving your children away from church? If so, what changes do you need to make?

11. What did you think of the quote "The last temptation is the final treason: to do the right thing for the wrong reason"? Are you guilty?

12. What is your reaction to the quote "The Cold War is over . . . and the East Germans won"? Do you agree that Americans are pushing their children too hard in sports and many other areas?

13. Do you push your children too hard? What are your real motives in doing so?

14. Are you constantly goading your husband on to success? Why is it so important for him to climb higher and higher, earning more and more money? Is it about him? Or about you?

15. How did you respond to the story of the young beauty queen, who really did get the life we all signed up for?

Digging Deeper

- Read Isaiah 61:1–4 and 9:
  What was Isaiah called to do?

  As a follower of Christ, you have the same call. What does God promise to those who fulfill that call?

  Is there a promise to our descendants?

- Read Jeremiah 33:6–9:
What will God do for his people?

  What will be the result of God's blessing?

  Who gets the praise in verse 9?

  Turn this passage into a prayer for your family.

- Meditate on Psalm 78:1–8:
What are we to recall?

  Who are we to tell?

  What will be the results of telling our children about God's faithfulness?

Look up the following passages and note what you discover about children/inheritance:

Psalm 127:3–5

Deuteronomy 6:3–12

Deuteronomy 11:16–21

Deuteronomy 30:19

Joshua 14:9

Isaiah 44:2–5

Isaiah 49:25

Isaiah 59:21

Psalm 25:12–14

Acts 3:25–26

Working It Into Your Life

Put together a Legacy Box for your children, filling it with tokens of significant spiritual milestones in your life. Be sure to include a letter that explains the significance of each item you place in the box. This will be a long-term project, but you might begin by acquiring a hope chest or something similar and placing a handful of items in it.

If you are part of a study group, bring either the letter or one of the items you plan to leave for your children.

Rewrite This Week's Key Verse

_____

_____

_____

_____

_____

Your Prayer in Response

_____

_____

_____

_____

_____

_____

_____

_____

_____

_____

Heavenly Father, I thank you for the gift of my children. I know they are my true legacy—the only thing I will leave behind on this earth when I depart. And I know that the most valuable inheritance I can leave for them is a spiritual one. Holy Spirit, I ask you to quicken my spirit whenever I get caught up in the daily grind and start losing sight of what is of eternal significance. Help me to focus less on how much my children are accomplishing and more on their heart condition. My family isn't perfect, but they are a blessing. Help me to always remember that. Amen.

I signed up to
make a difference

CHAPTER TEN

I Signed Up to Make a Difference

Simon, Simon, Satan has asked to sift you as wheat. But I have
prayed for you, Simon, that your faith may not fail. And when
you have turned back, strengthen your brothers.

Luke 22:31–32

Unlike so many, we do not peddle the word of God for profit.
On the contrary, in Christ we speak before God with sincerity,
like men sent from God.

2 Corinthians 2:17

Recently I visited the campus of Wheaton College and toured the
Billy Graham museum. What an incredibly moving experience
it was to survey Dr. Graham's life and ponder how mightily one
person can be used in the kingdom of God. What a difference
one man can make! My editor, Steve Laube, was with me. Just
before entering the museum we had finished an "important"

discussion about how I could sell more books. When we turned the corner into the first display area, I suddenly felt incredibly small, not to mention small-minded, so I turned to him and said, "Please smack me upside my head! What was I thinking? It's about faithfulness! It's not about how many books I sell or how many people attend my conferences! It's about faithfulness! I just want to be faithful!"

He solemnly promised to remind me of this insight on a routine basis in the future. We continued our tour of the museum, continued standing in awe of this giant of the faith. As we walked out the door, Steve turned to me and said, "There was a woman in our church who continuously prayed through the church directory, one family at a time. Every once in a while, we'd get a note from her saying, 'I prayed for you today.' She did it for years. She was faithful too, Donna, even though no one is going to build a museum in her honor."

It reminded me of a woman at a church I once attended. She had volunteered in the nursery for twenty-three years. Twenty-three years of caring for other people's two-year-olds so they could enjoy the morning worship. I doubt they'll ever erect a statue of her. The most faithful servant I've ever personally known was Dr. William Miller. In 1919, he sailed for Persia (now called Iran). He spent the next forty-three years as an itinerant evangelist, journeying from village to village, sharing Christ with the Muslims of that land. In all those years he saw only a small number of converts. He never built a huge ministry, never hosted large crusades. He didn't lead thousands to Christ, but he was faithful.

After he retired and returned to the United States, he continued laboring tirelessly on behalf of Muslims for another forty-plus years: writing books and pamphlets that explained the Gospel in terms they could understand; corresponding with Muslim seekers and converts from around the world; telling everyone who would listen about the desperate need to take the light of Christ to these lost souls. Twice each year, for twenty-nine years, he hosted the Fellowship of Faith for Muslims (FFM) Day of Prayer. He continued hosting the event until he was 101, even though, for most of those years, the event attracted only a small number of die-hard participants. Toward the end of his lifetime the FFM prayer movement began to grow, and it was one of his greatest joys.

He touched my life profoundly—precisely *because* he wasn't successful by the world's standards yet he persevered anyway.

He was faithful.

THE MEASURE OF FAITHFULNESS

The problem with faithfulness, of course, is that we're not quite sure how to measure it. We think if we're truly faithful, we will automatically be successful. And how do we measure success? By achievement. By numbers. By crowds and money. By the volume of approval and applause generated. We want tangible proof for all the world to see that God is blessing us. But we're back to square one: How do we define blessing?

I took a much-needed break from writing yesterday and spent the day with my friend Kathleen. For the past eight years she has taught a community-wide women's Bible study, sponsored by an Evangelical Free church, hosted at a Southern Baptist church, but attended by women from all denominations, from Catholic to charismatic. She is an incredibly gifted Bible teacher. Yet the number of women who attend has steadily dwindled in recent years rather than steadily increasing.

Frankly, I hadn't noticed, because when I show up for women's Bible study, I'm glued to my chair. More accurately, God's got me nailed to my chair, if you know what I mean. Since I travel many weekends throughout the year, conducting women's retreats, I often spend Sunday at airports rather than church. So Kathleen's teaching has been a major source of spiritual food for me. I'm always amazed at how God will speak through her exactly what I need to hear on a particular day. I know you've had the same experience with your own pastor or favorite Bible teacher.

I'm quite certain there are dozens of other women who feel the same way about Kathleen's teaching. So is God blessing her ministry, even though the number of women in attendance isn't skyrocketing? Is she successful? Is her life making a difference? She's certainly making a difference in my life.

We all want our lives to count for something. We want to make a difference. But so many of us were taught by the church that the only way to make a difference is to "get it right." If only we could live out the life everyone signed up for, then people around us would want to become Christians too. That's certainly true. There *are* people God has called to be glorious, shining lights in a dark world, like the beautiful young woman I described in the previous chapter. I know God works through her in a powerful way to inspire other young women to pursue holiness and personal purity. Her life is so blessed, who wouldn't want to be like her?

But since you've chosen to read a book entitled *This Isn't the Life I Signed Up For,* I suspect you're wondering if there is any way an ordinary woman like you can make a difference too. I've got great news for you. Do you know what happens when God takes your mess and adds a little age to it? Watch this:

Mess + age = Message

I often tease the women who've been blessed with great lives. "See that! You didn't make a mess, so you're just getting old. It's we mess makers who've got a message!" Actually, that's not true. We *all* have a message! Some can speak a message of God's abundant blessing. Others, like me, can speak a message of God's abundant mercy. The world needs to hear both messages preached loud and clear.

Philippians 2:14–16 encourages mess makers that we too can be shining lights, but only when we stop complaining about the mess and choose to move forward in search of hope and healing:

> Do everything without complaining or arguing, so that you may become blameless and pure, children of God without fault in a crooked and depraved generation, in which you shine like stars in the universe as you hold out the word of life.

Our most powerful opportunities for ministry are often borne out of our mistakes, out of our brokenness, out of those things in our lives that we didn't sign up for.

I believe our most powerful opportunities for ministry are often borne out of our mistakes, out of our brokenness, out of those things in our lives that we didn't sign up for. Or things we signed up for, out of our own foolishness, but now wish we hadn't. I find it extraordinary that God wants to take the very things we *didn't sign up for* and use them for his glory. I know for certain that he has taken my broken places and made them the centerpiece of my ministry.

TURN AND STRENGTHEN YOUR BROTHERS

Surely you know the story of Joseph. (If not, read Genesis 37–50.) He didn't sign up to be sold into slavery by his brothers. He didn't sign up to be unjustly imprisoned. He didn't sign up to be forgotten and left rotting in a dungeon. Ultimately, however, God turned his life around, making him a ruler in Egypt and a shining light for all generations. In speaking to his brothers, who had caused him so much pain, he said, "You intended to harm me, but God intended it for good to accomplish what is now being done, the saving of many lives" (Genesis 50:20). Maybe people have intended to harm you; God intends to save many lives through you. Your pain can make a difference. It says in verse 21 that "he reassured them and spoke kindly to them." Having found hope and healing on the other side of brokenness, he was in a position to turn and strengthen his brothers.

This is the very thing Jesus instructed Peter to do.

> "Simon, Simon, Satan has asked to sift you as wheat. But I have prayed for you, Simon, that your faith may not fail. And when you have turned back, strengthen your brothers" (Luke 22:31).

Did Jesus promise to stop Satan from picking on Peter? No. Did he say he would prevent Peter from failing? No. Did he tell Peter nothing bad would ever happen to him? No. Quite the contrary. Jesus said, in essence, "You're going to be tested beyond your limits, and you're going to blow it big time. Then you'll probably spend some time beating yourself up about it. But when you're done wallowing in regret, get up and use it for good."

God handpicked you, knowing every mistake you would ever make.

Isn't it amazing that Jesus handpicked Peter, knowing in advance every mistake he would ever make? Why? Because he knew that when Peter turned back, he would be in a position to effectively strengthen his brothers. God handpicked you, knowing every mistake you would ever make. He's not asking you to live a perfect life. He's asking you to turn and strengthen your brothers. He wants to turn your mess into a message.

The woman who didn't sign up for a painful childhood can turn and strengthen others who've lived through the same pain. She can put her arms around another woman and say, "Listen. It happened to me too. I'm not glad about it, but here's how God got me through to the other side." Or she can make it her mission to spare children from the kind of pain she endured. Perhaps by becoming a child advocate, campaigning for tougher sentences for child abusers. She can teach Sunday school and seek to be a positive force in the life of children. Or maybe she can simply reach out to latchkey children in her neighborhood.

The woman who didn't sign up for disappointing relationships can teach others the power of forgiveness, providing support to women who are struggling in their marriages or who've been hurt through divorce or other relational heartache.

The woman who didn't sign up to make foolish choices can serve as living proof that God gives fresh starts. I'll never forget one of the most powerful closing ceremonies I've ever conducted at a women's retreat. A very refined middle-aged woman—a woman who was clearly a pillar in the church—walked up to the microphone and said, "I've been in this church for thirty years, and I've never told any of you this. When I was seventeen years old, I had a child out of wedlock and gave it up for adoption." As tears began streaming down her face, a pregnant teenage girl stood up in the back of the church and walked forward. As they stood there embracing, everyone in the room knew that young woman's life was changed forever. She saw with her own eyes that her mistake didn't have to be the end of the world. The woman standing before her was living proof of hope and healing.

The woman who didn't sign up for disappointment with God—who perhaps has endured personal tragedy—has a unique opportunity to minister hope and healing to those facing a similar crisis. Whether it's a child with birth defects or the premature loss of a loved one, there's no shortage of hurting people who need to be strengthened.

The possibilities are endless. For every heartache known to humankind, there is someone qualified to bring hope and healing because they've already lived through it. As it says in 2 Corinthians 1:3–4:

> Praise be to the God and Father of our Lord Jesus Christ, the Father of compassion and the God of all comfort, who comforts us in all our troubles, so that we can comfort those in any trouble with the comfort we ourselves have received from God.

SINCERE FAITH

My life verse is 2 Corinthians 4:7: "But we have this treasure in jars of clay to show that this all-surpassing power is from God and not from us." I firmly believe the world doesn't need to see how perfect we are. It needs to see how powerful God is. People don't need to see how Christians never have any problems and never make any mistakes. They need to see how God is bigger than our problems and more powerful than our mistakes.

Another of my favorite passages is 2 Corinthians 2:17: "Unlike so many, we do not peddle the word of God for profit. On the contrary, in Christ we speak before God with sincerity, like men sent from God."

In the original Greek, the word *sincerity*, or sincere faith, literally means "without wax." During New Testament times, clay pots were big business. They were like first-century Tupperware— used for hauling and storing everything imaginable. Now, here's the important point. Each jar of clay was handmade, and it was inevitable that there would be some kind of crack or flaw somewhere in it. Everyone knew about the cracks. But since it was big business, the people selling the clay pots would cover the cracks with wax. It was all a game.

In the same way, we have this treasure—the radiance and glory of the living God—but we have it in a jar of clay. Each of us is handmade by God, completely unique. But since we live in a fallen world, where our fellow jars of clay routinely bump into us, some cracks are inevitable. And here's what I want you to grab hold of: Everyone knows about the cracks! So why waste time covering them up?

What's the number one reason non-Christians give for not attending church? "They're all a bunch of hypocrites!" See? They know about the cracks! They know about the wax! They know it's all a game, and they'd rather play something more fun, like golf, on a Sunday morning.

It's time to get real. It's time to strip off the wax and be honest enough to admit we're just jars of clay, like everyone else, and we have our share of cracks. We've faced heartaches and hard times. This isn't the life we signed up for . . . but! Here's the important part: We're finding hope and healing.

That's what we can offer the world.

SHARING ISN'T SPILLING

The young pregnant girl mentioned above didn't find hope and healing by looking at perfect church ladies. She found hope and healing when one of those seemingly perfect church ladies had the courage to strip off the wax. Will you have the courage to strip off the layers of wax you've spent years building up?

Now I need to add a word about balance, because I've been guilty of being out of balance myself. We don't need to share every sordid detail of our life story with everyone we meet. Again, it comes back to why we're doing what we're doing. It benefits no one for you to spill the beans to everyone who gets within a mile of you. What are your motives for sharing your broken places? Are you looking for sympathy? Attention? Are you looking to one-up someone else's heartache? To say, "Oh, yeah, that's nothing! My life is way worse than yours."

One of the wrong motives God recently showed me is that very often I would "expose my cracks" to people *so that* they would make allowances for me. I wanted them to say, "Well, poor Donna. Now that we know her full story, we won't expect her to behave appropriately. No matter how outlandish she gets, we'll just excuse her for it." (That way, even though my behavior deserved disapproval, I could still get some approval thanks to the sympathy factor. The Bucket Lady rears her ugly head again!) The only legitimate motive for sharing our pain is to bring hope and healing to others.

Even when our motives are right, we still need to be sensitive to how and where we share. It's taken me a long time to figure out that sharing isn't the same as spilling. Being raw isn't the only way to be real. We must share truth in a way that doesn't defile us, our loved ones, or our listeners. As we listen to God, he'll give us the right words to share at the right time with the right people. He is far more eager to redeem our broken places than we are to have them redeemed.

Jesus said, "If I be lifted up . . . [I] will draw all men unto me" (John 12:32, KJV). If we want to make a difference, we will share our lives in a way that Jesus is lifted up. The punch line of every testimony must be "But God!"

I was in pain, but God . . .

I made foolish choices, but God . . .

I couldn't find my way, but God . . .

It's not about us. It's about God. Remember that, and you're halfway healed.

President Calvin Coolidge once said, "You can't do everything at once, but you can do something at once." Begin today. Allow God to take those things in your life you didn't sign up for and use them for the saving of someone's life. Your life can make a difference.

I leave you with these words of encouragement, posted on my office wall:

> Joy alone is a healer, and you can have it in the darkest hour if you will force your soul to rise to Me in worship and adoration. Bring your sorrow, and watch for the sunrise of the resurrection. Yea, verily there comes always a resurrection—a morning when hope is re-born and life finds a new beginning. Let his peace flow in you like a river, carrying away all the poison of painful memories and bringing to you a fresh, clear stream of pure life and restoring thoughts. This is not the end. Press on. The goal line is out ahead, and you may yet be a winner in the race of life.[1]

GROWTH GUIDE

Key Points to Remember

- One life can make a difference.
- The problem with faithfulness is that we're not quite sure how to measure it. We think if we're truly faithful, we will automatically be successful.
- Making a difference has nothing to do with success; it has to do with faithfulness.
- Many Christians are taught that the only way to make a difference is to have the life everyone signed up for so people around us will want to be like us.

---

[1] Roberts, *Come Away, My Beloved*, 26–27.

- When God takes your mess and adds a little age to it, you've got a message! Mess + age = Message!

- We *all* have a message. Some can speak a message of God's abundant blessing. Others can speak a message of God's abundant mercy. The world needs to hear both messages preached loud and clear.

- Often, our most powerful opportunities for ministry are born out of our mistakes, out of our brokenness, out of those things in our lives that we didn't sign up for. Or things we inadvertently signed up for, out of our own foolishness, but now wish we hadn't.

- People don't need to see how Christians never have any problems and never make any mistakes; they need to see how God is bigger than our problems and more powerful than our mistakes.

- If we want to make a difference, we will share our lives in such a way that Jesus is lifted up. The punch line of every testimony must be "But God!"

Application Questions

1. Do you believe your life has made a difference? In what ways?

2. Do you focus more on results or faithfulness?

3. Tell about someone you know who demonstrates quiet faithfulness. Someone who will never have a statue erected in his/her honor.

4. Is there someone who has touched your life profoundly, precisely because they weren't successful according to the world's definition yet they persevered anyway?

5. Were you taught that the only way to make a difference as a Christian is to live such a perfect life that people around you will want to become like you?

6. Realistically speaking, are you more qualified to speak a message of God's abundant blessing or God's abundant mercy?

7. Are you content with the message God has given you or would you rather have someone else's? (Some women who've been richly blessed apologize for not having a "testimony," while women with a "testimony" envy the women who were blessed!)

8. What areas of brokenness in your life might God be able to transform from a mess into a message?

9. God is calling you to "turn and strengthen your [sisters]" (see Luke 22:32). Ask him to show you who, specifically, you can impart strength to.

10. Which are you more inclined to emphasize: the fact that Christians shouldn't make mistakes or that God is bigger than our mistakes? Try to answer honestly. You might ask your family or the non-Christians in your life what THEY think you emphasize!

11. How much "wax" are you wearing to cover up the cracks in your life?

12. What is one step you can take, right now, to begin removing some of the layers of wax?

13. In your opinion, how do you distinguish between sharing and spilling?

14. Have you been guilty of spilling rather than sharing? In what situations?

Digging Deeper

- Read the life of Joseph, from Genesis 30 to 50:
  List the broken places in his life.

  How did God work through those broken places?

Working It Into Your Life

1. Write out your testimony, without wax. Be prepared to share it with your small group. Pray, asking God to open up other opportunities for you to share, either one-on-one or perhaps in a group setting.
2. Watch the movie *It's a Wonderful Life*, even if it's not Christmastime! Think about the difference one life can make.

Rewrite One of This Week's Key Verses

_____

_____

_____

_____

_____

_____

Your Prayer in Response

_____

_____

_____

_____

_____

_____

_____

_____

_____

_____

Heavenly Father, I am so thankful that one life really can make a difference. Forgive me for those times when I have wanted to shield my heart under layers of wax. Grant me the courage to be sincere. Holy Spirit, I pray that you would open my eyes to see the broken, hurting vessels all around me, and show me how I can comfort them with the comfort you have given me. I want my life to make a difference for Jesus' sake. Amen.

A Note to Leaders

Dear Leader:

I want to personally thank you for choosing this book as a tool for the spiritual growth of the women God has entrusted to your care. I pray that it will enrich your life as you teach this material to others. The study portions of the book are designed to make the material as self-taught as possible. When your group gathers, you can simply recap the week's lesson using the Key Points as your outline. Be sure to add your own personal insights and illustrations to bring life to the study.

I would encourage you to spur the women on in Scripture memory. I truly believe it is a powerful tool for transforming our minds and ultimately our lives. Prior to class, I would encourage you to circle the Application Questions you want to be certain the class discusses as a group. You may not get to every question, but using this approach, you'll be sure to get to the ones you feel are most crucial to the study.

I've provided the Digging Deeper section primarily for personal use. Some women will take the time for this; others will not. And that's fine. I would instruct the women that this section of each chapter is optional and will not be used in class.

By all means, strongly encourage the women to write out their prayers. This is such a wonderful spiritual discipline and may eventually inspire some women to begin keeping a full-fledged prayer journal. Each week, encourage some of the women to read their written prayers aloud to the class. This can be a tremendous blessing to the entire group.

In addition to the discussion material for each chapter, I have provided suggestions for group activities in the Discussion Leader's Guide that follows this note. I would strongly encourage you to READ AHEAD in case there are items the women need to bring to class in order to participate more effectively. Then you can remind them what they'll need for the coming week. Also, you will have to do some advance preparation for each lesson. You might want to sit down right now, along with your calendar, and note what you will need for each week.

At your first meeting, be sure to emphasize to the group that although this is in many ways an individual journey, you will be taking it together so you can help one another along. It will be helpful for the women to remember that they are surrounded by the "presence of many witnesses" who have walked paths different in context but identical in the concept of conforming us to the image of Christ. Each journey is as significant and distinct as our fingerprints! If you have accepted God's glorious plan of salvation through his Son, Jesus Christ, then all roads on your journey lead into the everlasting arms of our heavenly Father.

Women should not compare their life journeys to one another so as to feel inferior or superior, but rather should rejoice in how far each one has come and how each is unique.

Most people are drawn to a study for a reason. Perhaps they have many unanswered questions as to why certain things have happened in their lives. Others will attend because they have seen friendships tested, often to the breaking point. Many are living through trials they never would have signed up for. Encourage each woman to share with the group why she has chosen to take this particular class.

This study is an open invitation for us to turn over circumstances we may never have signed up for to God, who can bring something beautiful out of the rubble of our lives. Encourage each woman to affirm her decision, and her commitment to the group, to move forward in search of hope and healing.

Concerning prayer, find out if there are members in your group who may not be accustomed to or who are uncomfortable praying out loud in a group. (Some women have left study groups over this issue.) Make an effort to reassure everyone involved that while everyone is encouraged to pray, no one will be pressured to pray aloud.

Another issue that may arise for some women is hesitation about writing their feelings or circumstances in a book that could be discovered by someone else. You might suggest that they use symbols for things they do not want to write out in full, or write out those more personal issues on a separate piece of paper that can be disposed of after the class. In any case, be sure to emphasize that it is VERY important for them to write out their answers.

Lastly, ask all of the women to commit to one another that they will respect each other's privacy—that the information shared in the room must stay in the room. Emphasize this as strongly as you know how! If any person's trust is violated, everyone's trust will be violated and the effectiveness of your group will be greatly diminished.

It is my earnest prayer that this study will move everyone who participates in it one step closer to the life they signed up for!

His vessel,
Donna Partow
www.donnapartow.com

Discussion Leader's Guide

CHAPTER 1: I DIDN'T SIGN UP FOR THIS LIFE

Discussion

Ask those participating in the study whether they are ready to get real, as it suggests in the first chapter. Ask for suggestions from the group as to what that could mean for all who participate in the study.

Suggested Activities

1. *Game Show Skit*—two contestants answering questions: one always gives the honest answer while the other always gives the "correct" answer or the expected answer. The purpose of this would be to illustrate the differences in our perspectives and how those perspectives affect our choices and ultimately our lives.

2. *Take a group photograph* and get enough copies so that each member can have one. Ask all the members if they are willing to commit themselves to this journey and to

helping their fellow group members along their journey to hope and healing. If they are willing, tell them to tape the group photo inside their book as a reminder that they have made a real commitment to real people. Talk about the importance of remaining faithful to that commitment even when it's inconvenient or difficult.

3. *Play Truth or Prayer* (instead of Truth or Dare). Take turns sharing one of the top things you didn't sign up for in life. Then spend time in prayer about what others have shared. After the group has finished the book, come back to the things that were shared the first day and ask everyone how God has changed their perspective.

4. *Bring a stack of DVDs* to class, or a list of familiar movie titles representing several kinds of films. Review them briefly one at a time, illustrating the unrealistic lives people sign up for:

- *Action flick:* We are powerful. We can "stick it to" the people who deserve it. We finally take charge of things and make the life we want for ourselves. Nothing and nobody will stand in our way. We are in control!

- *Romantic chick flick:* We have the relationship we've always deserved, with a knight on a white horse who is perfectly strong, capable, and sensitive to our needs.

- *Lighthearted comedy:* We have an easy life where money is no problem, fun is the goal, and it doesn't matter if our entertainment ends up hurting someone else. We make all sorts of cutting remarks to everyone we don't like, but we are so witty that no one takes offense. Life is a game, right?

- *Intense drama/thriller:* People finally see our life for the crisis it is and feel sorry for us accordingly. The world stops for our pain.

- *Family movie:* We discover that we really were born to wonderful parents and were accidentally switched in the hospital. We are joyfully reunited with the picture-perfect family we've always known we should have had.

CHAPTER 2: I DIDN'T SIGN UP FOR A PAINFUL CHILDHOOD

Discussion

You will note that I have "stepped up to the plate" by allowing readers to glimpse my childhood, early life, and family. Self-disclosure is the hallmark of intimacy. If you disclose truth about your own life, it often opens up others to share as well. Take a poll to see who in the room actually did have the kind of childhood someone would want to sign up for. It can sometimes be helpful to recognize that people who were blessed with solid childhoods still grow up to experience suffering. As the discussions about suffering continue, we need to recognize that just as a rough childhood doesn't mean you are destined to live in tragedy, a great childhood doesn't mean you are destined to a life of ease either. As parents, we need to provide a solid childhood for our kids *without* sowing in them the lie that this guarantees a perfect life. A solid Christian childhood gives a person the tools to live well in a world that includes enough suffering for all. Are we giving our kids those tools or just a "happy" childhood?

Suggested Activities

1. Recruit two women (in advance) to prepare and act out the "Cannibals at Lunch" skit.
2. Have each woman write a one-page description of her

childhood and invite those who would like to, to read it aloud.

3. Invite the ladies (in advance) to bring in photos of themselves at very young ages, and play a game to see if they can guess who's who. Then ask each woman to explain how her friends or classmates would have described her back then. How about her family? How did she see herself? How did God see her?

4. Ask the women (in advance) to bring in their high school yearbooks. Invite everyone to share something about that period in her life.

5. Form a Chain of Lies. Cut black construction paper into strips and bring it to class. Pass several strips out to each woman, asking her to write her "destructive seeds/lies" on each strip (one lie per strip). Then staple the lies together to demonstrate how each lie we believe intersects with the lies believed by the women around us. Hang the chains over a cross or place them at the foot of a cross. Alternatively, place the paper chains in a fire-safe container, take them outdoors, and burn them.

6. Bring in flower seeds and small planters. Allow the women to plant something beautiful to replace the destructive seeds in their lives.

7. This is the ideal time to establish prayer partners. Phone partnerships are the easiest for most people, since physically getting together can be difficult. Suggest that those participating pick a time when they are least likely to be uninterrupted and decide who will place the call. They may agree to pray together daily or weekly. If praying on the phone is uncomfortable, explain that they can ease this discomfort by sitting in a quiet environment just like they would while praying alone or conversing with a friend.

Instruct them to limit the amount of time spent talking before praying, since this is the greatest pitfall for most phone prayer partners! Exchange greetings and express specific prayer requests that need explanation. Decide who will pray first and then go for it!

You can draw names out of a hat to set up partnerships or choose another method that works for the women in your group. Prayer partnerships are especially helpful because they naturally roll over into accountability relationships as you follow up with one another on the concerns you've been praying about. Try it, and see if God doesn't richly bless your group.

CHAPTER 3: I DIDN'T SIGN UP FOR DISAPPOINTING RELATIONSHIPS

Discussion

This week's lesson was, in many ways, the most intensely personal you will encounter throughout the journey. When we speak of agonizing forgiveness, we are getting to the deepest pain a woman can experience. Give the women freedom to share—or not share—who they are struggling to forgive. If anyone has had a breakthrough, by all means, let everyone join in the celebration.

Suggested Activity

If you feel the women in your group can handle it, set up a mock courtroom. You will need to assign someone to play the judge and another to stand in the place of the heavenly Father. Let each woman take turns walking up to the judge and presenting her list. (Do not read these aloud.) Then have her turn the list over to her heavenly Father.

CHAPTER 4: I DIDN'T SIGN UP TO MAKE FOOLISH CHOICES

Discussion

Discuss obvious life situations where choices need to be made as well as the logical consequences of those choices: If you don't water a plant, it will die; if you don't grocery shop, you won't have any food to eat; if you don't fill up your gas tank, your car won't run. These simple everyday choices have obvious outcomes. Tie this to the fact that we constantly live with the consequences of our choices, even when the outcome is NOT quite so obvious.

Suggested Activities

1. Remind the women, in advance, to bring in their stuffed sheep. Let each woman talk about her sheep, along with the "bleating sheep" it represents.
2. Bring in construction paper, scissors, glue, and cotton balls. Let the women make their own sheep, as many as needed to represent consequences to actions in their lives.
3. Do a Window Closing Ceremony in the home (or classroom) where your group meets. Gather by an open window and spend a few moments in individual prayers of confession and repentance.

CHAPTER 5: I DIDN'T SIGN UP FOR DISAPPOINTMENT WITH GOD

Discussion

Bring a baseball glove to class. Place it on the floor in the middle of the room where everyone can see it. Discuss the difference that would come into our lives if we lived like the glove, moving only in response to the hand of God inside. The glove does not exhaust itself trying to catch balls. It simply moves as the hand inside does, and the success or failure of each attempt belongs to the hand, not the glove, so false guilt is removed. At the same time, the glove needs to be soft and pliable, and it must not slip off the hand or it becomes useless.

Encourage the women to share which passage of Scripture they chose to meditate on or which member of the Great Hall of Faith they researched more fully.

Suggested Activities

1. Meet in the kitchen rather than in your usual spot, and make homemade bread (if you have someone experienced enough to lead the exercise) or simply let the class join in as you load the ingredients into a bread machine.[1] Either way, you can all enjoy the aroma as it bakes and then conclude your session by eating fresh bread. Be sure to bring along some butter or jam! Place slices of bread on some plates and pieces of chewing gum on others. Let the women choose which they prefer and ask them to explain their choice.

2. Make a Bible promise book. Have a creative woman in the class bring enough craft supplies, along with a design concept. (You could have all the women pitch in to cover the cost of supplies.) Each member of the class can carefully write her favorite Bible promise in each of the other members' books. If time and space allows and women are so inclined, they can contribute more than one verse to their classmates.

[1] Substitute quick bread for a shorter activity.

CHAPTER 6: I SIGNED UP FOR HAPPINESS

Discussion

Galatians 6:2–5 says that we should carry one another's burdens but that each one should carry his own load. Explain the difference between an unusual burden that requires help from others to carry and your normal God-assigned load that is your responsibility.

Invite the women to share their lists of the top twenty things they have to be thankful for.

Suggested Activities

1. Perhaps you can find a giant boulder near where your class meets. Stand next to the boulder with a knapsack that has a few small rocks in it. Talk about the contrast in terms of burdens.
2. If weather permits, go outside and let the women gather bags full of rocks. (You could supply shopping bags; double-bag if necessary.) In advance, assign each woman a specific number of rocks to gather. Next, have the women exchange bags so they can experience carrying heavy or lighter loads. Talk about whether or not it is fair if one woman gathers ten rocks, and then asks another woman with five to carry hers. (Another option would be to have several women prepare this in advance as a skit.)
3. If women have brought in magnifying glasses or pictures, allow them time to illustrate to the class the concept of focusing on something and how we all tend to magnify certain things or issues in our lives.

CHAPTER 7: I SIGNED UP FOR GREAT HEALTH

Discussion

You (or someone who is willing) might come in to class with a crutch and a wrap on your foot, a sling on your arm, a bandage on your head, or other demonstration of injury. Perhaps several women could put together a skit talking to each other about their various ailments and taking great delight in sharing the gory details!

Take an inventory of the class (these ailments may be current or chronic or occasional):

Who has a:
- headache?
- sore throat?
- toothache?
- stomachache?
- earache?

Who has aching:
- hands?
- feet?
- legs?
- shoulders?
- hips?
- back?

Who has:
- skin irritations?
- more serious ailments?

Pray over these areas. Pray with and for each other.

Suggested Activities

1. In advance, have one of the women prepare a series of stretching exercises in which everyone who would like to can participate. You might encourage the women to wear comfortable clothing this week.
2. See if there is any interest in participating in a group fast for the upcoming week. If so, make out a list of specific prayer issues you plan to focus on during the fast.

CHAPTER 8: I SIGNED UP FOR LOVE

Discussion

Gather the lyrics to several popular love songs. Discuss whether or not they capture the essence of biblical love. If you have access to a CD player, you might play short segments of various love songs.

Suggested Activity

Conduct the Bucket Surrendering Ceremony.

CHAPTER 9: I SIGNED UP FOR THE PERFECT LITTLE FAMILY

Discussion

Discuss the type of legacy you want to leave your family.

Suggested Activity

Invite the women to share items from their Legacy Boxes. Call several women ahead of time to be sure some are prepared to share.

CHAPTER 10: I SIGNED UP TO MAKE A DIFFERENCE

Discussion

Contact several women in advance and ask them if they would be willing to share their testimonies. Encourage them to WRITE IT OUT and time it. (Otherwise, five-minute testimonies can last for twenty minutes!) If you really want this exercise to be effective, you might get together with the women beforehand to go over what they will share with the group.

Suggested Activities

1. If not included in today's schedule, plan a farewell brunch or other special event to conclude the study next week.
2. Discuss what the women would like to study next. Peruse study books in advance so that you can make informed suggestions. (May I suggest using one of my books: *Becoming a Vessel God Can Use* [Bethany House, 2004], *Becoming the Woman I Want to Be* [Bethany House, 2004], and *Becoming the Woman God Wants Me to Be* [Revell, 2008].)
3. Conduct the Broken Places Ceremony:
   a. Prior to class, gather two or three lightweight terracotta pots, a hammer, a thick pillar candle (sized to fit under one of the pots), enough taper candles for each woman in the group, a lighter, two or three baskets, and a flashlight.
   b. In class, recap the teaching from chapter 10 about broken places.
   c. Place the lighted candle under one of the terracotta pots. (If you can darken the room, so much the better—give a flashlight to the person who will read the Scripture passage.)

d. Have someone read selected portions of the passage from Judges 7, where Gideon's soldiers smash their jars of clay.

e. Using the hammer, crack the terracotta pot just enough for the light to shine through its broken places.

f. Next, smash a second terracotta pot into enough small pieces for each woman in your group to receive one. (If you have a very large group, you may want to do this in advance.) Place the broken pieces into baskets.

g. Distribute a broken piece of pottery to each woman.

h. Now begin to pray, asking God to show women the broken places in their lives. Instruct them to come forward and lay down their broken places on the altar (or at the foot of a cross, depending on what you have available in your particular environment).

i. Play or sing "The Potter's Hand" (from the *Shout to the Lord 2000* CD) or other appropriate song. If you have a worship leader in your group, ask her in advance to be prepared to lead the women in worship.

j. Hand each woman a candle as she surrenders her broken piece, and allow her to light it from the central candle.

k. Be sure to end the ceremony on a positive note. Women will be moved by this exercise, and there may be tears. But their broken places are OLD news. Today, they have heard the GOOD news that God can bring something wonderful out of their pain. After allowing ample time for the women to reflect on their broken places, invite them to shift their attention from their own pain to women in their community who may have experienced (or who are currently experiencing) the same brokenness. These women may not know God and therefore cannot experience hope and healing. Remind your group that they have an incredible opportunity to participate in God's plan of redemption by reaching out to comfort others with the comfort they have received. Not only can they find hope and healing, but God wants to work through them to bring hope and healing to others.

1. Encourage the women to take their candles home and light them from time to time, as a reminder that the purpose of this exercise is not to concentrate on our brokenness but to remind us that God's glory can shine through our lives to a darkened world.

4. I Didn't Sign Up to Make Foolish Choices

Matthew 7:1–2

Do not judge, or you too will be judged. For in the same way you judge others, you will be judged, and with the measure you use, it will be measured to you.

This Isn't the Life I Signed Up For, Donna Partow

---

5. I Didn't Sign Up for Disappointment With God

2 Peter 1:3–4

His divine power has given us everything we need for life and godliness through our knowledge of him who called us by his own glory and goodness. Through these he has given us his very great and precious promises, so that through them you may participate in the divine nature and escape the corruption in the world caused by evil desires.

This Isn't the Life I Signed Up For, Donna Partow

---

6. I Signed Up for Happiness

Matthew 11:28–30

Come to me, all you who are weary and burdened, and I will give you rest. Take my yoke upon you and learn from me, for I am gentle and humble in heart, and you will find rest for your souls. For my yoke is easy and my burden is light.

This Isn't the Life I Signed Up For, Donna Partow

---

1. I Didn't Sign Up for This Life

Deuteronomy 30:19–20

This day I call heaven and earth as witnesses against you that I have set before you life and death, blessings and curses. Now choose life, so that you and your children may live and that you may love the Lord your God, listen to his voice, and hold fast to him.

This Isn't the Life I Signed Up For, Donna Partow

---

2. I Didn't Sign Up for a Painful Childhood

John 8:44

When he lies, he speaks his native language, for he is a liar and the father of lies.

Galatians 5:15

If you keep on biting and devouring each other, watch out or you will be destroyed by each other.

This Isn't the Life I Signed Up For, Donna Partow

---

3. I Didn't Sign Up for Disappointing Relationships

Matthew 6:14–15

For if you forgive men when they sin against you, your heavenly Father will also forgive you. But if you do not forgive men their sins, your Father will not forgive your sins.

Hebrews 12:15

See to it that no one misses the grace of God and that no bitter root grows up to cause trouble and defile many.

This Isn't the Life I Signed Up For, Donna Partow

1 Peter 2:9-10

But you are a chosen people, a royal priesthood, a holy nation, a people belonging to God, that you may declare the praises of him who called you out of darkness into his wonderful light. Once you were not a people, but now you are the people of God; once you had not received mercy, but now you have received mercy.

This Isn't the Life I Signed Up For, Donna Partow

Ephesians 3:20-21

Now to him who is able to do immeasurably more than all we ask or imagine, according to his power that is at work within us, to him be glory in the church and in Christ Jesus throughout all generations, for ever and ever! Amen.

This Isn't the Life I Signed Up For, Donna Partow

Philippians 2:14-16

Do everything without complaining or arguing, so that you may become blameless and pure, children of God without fault in a crooked and depraved generation, in which you shine like stars in the universe as you hold out the word of life—in order that I may boast on the day of Christ that I did not run or labor for nothing.

This Isn't the Life I Signed Up For, Donna Partow

10. I Signed Up to Make a Difference

Luke 22:31-32

Simon, Simon, Satan has asked to sift you as wheat. But I have prayed for you, Simon, that your faith may not fail. And when you have turned back, strengthen your brothers.

2 Corinthians 2:17

Unlike so many, we do not peddle the word of God for profit. On the contrary, in Christ we speak before God with sincerity, like men sent from God.

This Isn't the Life I Signed Up For, Donna Partow

7. I Signed Up for Great Health

Matthew 9:35

Jesus went through all the towns and villages, teaching in their synagogues, preaching the good news of the kingdom and healing every disease and sickness.

2 Corinthians 7:1

Since we have these promises, dear friends, let us purify ourselves from everything that contaminates body and spirit, perfecting holiness out of reverence for God.

This Isn't the Life I Signed Up For, Donna Partow

8. I Signed Up for Love

Psalm 139:13-16

For you created my inmost being;
you knit me together in my mother's womb.
I praise you because I am fearfully and
	wonderfully made;
your works are wonderful,
I know that full well.
My frame was not hidden from you
	when I was made in the secret place.
(continued on back)

This Isn't the Life I Signed Up For, Donna Partow

9. I Signed Up for the Perfect Little Family

Psalm 112:1-2

Blessed is the [woman] who fears the Lord,
who finds great delight in his commands.
[Her] children will be mighty in the land;
the generation of the upright will be blessed.

This Isn't the Life I Signed Up For, Donna Partow

When I was woven together in the depths of the earth,
your eyes saw my unformed body.

Jeremiah 2:13

My people have committed two sins: They have forsaken me, the spring of living water, and have dug their own cisterns, broken cisterns that cannot hold water.

This Isn't the Life I Signed Up For, Donna Partow

AFFIRMATION

I can either magnify God or magnify my problems. I choose to magnify God. (Psalm 69:30–31)

This Isn't the Life I Signed Up For, Donna Partow

AFFIRMATION

I'm not going to be afraid of anything today. Because God has not given me a spirit of fear but of love, power, and a sound mind. (2 Timothy 1:7)

This Isn't the Life I Signed Up For, Donna Partow

AFFIRMATION

Today I will know, firsthand, the love of Christ, which passes knowledge, and I will be filled with the fullness of God. (Ephesians 3:19)

This Isn't the Life I Signed Up For, Donna Partow

AFFIRMATION

The enemy may come against me one way; but he will be forced to flee from me seven ways! (Deuteronomy 28:7)

This Isn't the Life I Signed Up For, Donna Partow

AFFIRMATION

No weapon formed against me today will prosper. All those who rise up against me will fall. Every accusation made against me will be refuted. (Isaiah 54:17)

This Isn't the Life I Signed Up For, Donna Partow

AFFIRMATION

I know today will be a great day, because God's mercies are new every morning. (Lamentations 3:23)

This Isn't the Life I Signed Up For, Donna Partow

AFFIRMATION

I always choose to offer the sacrifice of praise and thanksgiving. (Hebrews 13:15) God inhabits praise. The enemy inhabits negativity. I choose God. And I choose to praise him.

This Isn't the Life I Signed Up For, Donna Partow

AFFIRMATION

I will remember: She who guards her mouth and her tongue keeps herself from trouble. (Proverbs 21:23)

This Isn't the Life I Signed Up For, Donna Partow

AFFIRMATION

I never complain, because it robs me—and everyone around me—of joy. Besides, the world doesn't need any more verbal pollution. (Philippians 2:14)

This Isn't the Life I Signed Up For, Donna Partow

AFFIRMATION

I never complain, because I refuse to whistle for the devil. (Philippians 2:14)

This Isn't the Life I Signed Up For, Donna Partow

AFFIRMATION

I have absolutely no regrets about my life. Everything that has happened to me, even the pain, will be redeemed and turned into something good. (Romans 8:28)

This Isn't the Life I Signed Up For, Donna Partow

AFFIRMATION

This family is blessed when we come in and blessed when we go out. (Deuteronomy 28:6)

This Isn't the Life I Signed Up For, Donna Partow

AFFIRMATION	AFFIRMATION	AFFIRMATION
I am becoming more and more like Jesus all the time: gracious, generous, anointed, and compassionate. I walk moment by moment in the power of the Holy Spirit. (2 Corinthians 3:17–18)	If people could sum me up in one word, I hope it would be *gracious*. I seek to always extend to others the same grace God has extended to me. (Ephesians 4:29–32)	I never curse or condemn anyone, because I want to keep God's blessings flowing into my life. (Luke 6:37)
This Isn't the Life I Signed Up For, Donna Partow	*This Isn't the Life I Signed Up For*, Donna Partow	*This Isn't the Life I Signed Up For*, Donna Partow
AFFIRMATION	AFFIRMATION	AFFIRMATION
I never judge anyone, because I know everyone is doing the best they can. (Matthew 7:1) And I don't know everyone's story.	I know that life and death are in the power of the tongue. I choose to make the words of my mouth and the meditation of my heart acceptable before God. (Psalm 19:14)	I never make excuses for my behavior. All that does is keep me stuck in my old ways. (1 John 1:8–9)
This Isn't the Life I Signed Up For, Donna Partow	*This Isn't the Life I Signed Up For*, Donna Partow	*This Isn't the Life I Signed Up For*, Donna Partow

Donna Partow

In this bestselling book, you will see that God can—and does—accomplish extraordinary things through ordinary people, imperfections and all. Join Donna on a 10-week journey of hope, laughter, and transformation and discover new confidence and significance as you see how you can make a difference in your world.

Becoming a Vessel God Can Use

If you're like Donna, you've tried a lot of ways to improve your life. Enough with good intentions—now is the time for results! With an easy-to-use plan for better spiritual and physical health, Donna offers a 90-day journey to renewal and becoming the woman you want to be. What do you have to lose—besides bad habits and perhaps a few excess pounds?

Becoming the Woman I Want to Be

With inspiration and practical direction, Donna helps you walk the path toward better living in all areas of life—spiritual, emotional, physical, and relational. Through a holistic, 90-day guide, you will move to that goal with passion, purpose, and energy, growing in character today and becoming the woman God wants you to be.

Becoming the Woman God Wants Me to Be